Student To Millionaire: Mastering Real Estate Investment

SADANAND PUJARI

Published by SADANAND PUJARI, 2024.

Table of Contents

Copyright 1

About 2

Introduction 4

Deed 10

Title Insurance 15

Real Estate Documents Needing to Be Recorded 24

Property Rights Limitations 28

Promissory Notes Provisions 38

Mortgage Instrument 45

Does The Bank Own Part of My Home NO 58

Bankruptcy 64

Time Value of Money 70

Present Value 78

Present Value Months as Period 89

Future Value 92

Future Value Months As Period 101

Future Value vs Present Value 104

Present Value Annuity 108

Present Value Annuity Months as Period 117

Future Value Annuity 120

Future Value Annuity Months 128

Present Value Cash Flow Examples 131

Future Value Cash Flow Examples 140

Present Value Terms Used In Capital Budgeting 146

Net Present Value Assumptions 152

Future Value FV Multiple Forms of Calculation 154

Present Value (PV) Calculation – Multiple Ways 168

Future Value Compounded Annually vs Semi Annually 178

Present Value (PV) Decision Making 191

Present value Different Discount Rates Side by Side 202

Present Value Planning Scenario 209

Future Value of an Annuity 224

Future Value Uneven Investments 232

Present Value Annuity 240

Present Value Annuity Part 2 249

Uneven Payments 259

Future Value of a Collectible 270

Future Value of an Annuity 276

How Long to Double or Triple Investments 283

Estimate Stock Returns & Sale 294

Conclusion 303

Copyright

Copyright © 2024 by **SADANAND PUJARI**

All rights reserved. No part of this book may be reproduced, scanned, or distributed in any printed or electronic form without permission. Please do not participate in or encourage piracy of copyrighted materials in violation of the author's rights. Purchase only authorized editions.

Student To Millionaire: Mastering Real Estate Investment

From Campus To Cash Flow: Real Estate Investment Mastery

First Edition: Jun 2024

Book Design by **SADANAND PUJARI**

About

This Book will provide many useful tools for real estate investors and home buyers. Real estate investing in a complex topic for many reasons. Real estate is a large investment, often requiring a significant part of an individual's asset portfolio. Real estate investing often requires financing which increases the complexity. The reason for purchasing real estate varies greatly from person to person, some looking for a long-term home, others looking primarily for an investment, most wanting some mixture of both. Regulations also play a significant role in real estate investing decisions.

This Book will start out with the basics. We will discuss basic real estate terms because every specialized field will have terminology we need to understand to communicate well and make decisions.

Real estate transactions have many components and players involved. Once we understand the basic terminology, we will discuss how those components and players fit together for a real estate transaction to take place.

Because real estate is a long-term investment, we need to understand the time value of money concepts. This Book will provide a chapter explaining what time value of money concepts are and will demonstrate the tools needed to use time value of money concepts. We will learn how to use

Excel formulas to calculate present value, future value, payments, and interest rates.

Learners will understand different financing options. We will apply our time value of money concepts as we create amortization schedules and worksheets to help us analyze different financing options.

Introduction

Get ready because it's time to raise the stakes with real estate. Like with any other specialized area, real estate has its own specialized terms and definitions, terms and definitions, we need to understand in order to be able to properly communicate within the field, within the area, we're going to be starting off with some basic definitions, definitions, which you can find more information at Investopedia. So most of the definitions we look at, you may be able to find Investopedia and get more information there if you so choose. Started off with real property, so real property can be defined as land, everything permanently attached to it, and all of the interest benefits and rights inherent in the ownership of real estate.

So real property. Notice we're thinking here. The governing point or this central point is the land. Because remember, remember, when you're thinking about the real property, the land is the thing that we would think isn't going to be changing in basically human lifetimes. It's going to be the most constant component of real estate. Everything that we put onto the land, even though we're going to put in things that could be permanent structures such as buildings and homes and so on. Those are far less permanent than the land. You could take the building off of there. You can demolition to build into land is still going to be there. So that's going to be the anchoring kind of component. Generally, in our mind.

We're saying, okay, we've got the land and then we've got everything permanently attached to it. The things that we would most likely think of as being permanently attached to it would be something like the building, like a home or some other structure attached to it. And once again, even though we're calling it permanently attached to it, that means we can't easily move the home, Of course. But it doesn't mean that we can't, you know, take off the home. We can't destroy the home, demolish the home and put something on the land, the land being more constant. So when we're thinking about real property in terms of a home or something like that, we typically think of them as one unit. We think of what's going to be the cost of the land and in the structure that's going to be on it.

But it's useful to break them off for valuation purposes and other reasons, which we may do in future chapters, thinking of the land separate from, you know, the structure that's going to be on it also for depreciation purposes and whatnot. That building, Of course, or any structure we would expect to decline in value, have wear and tear applied to it, whereas the land we would expect to be constant. So land everything permanently attached to it and all the interest benefits and rights inherent in the ownership of the real estate. So all the rights that we would have from the ownership of it. So then we have real estate as opposed to real property.

So real estate is defined as land at above and below the earth's surface, including all things permanently attached to it. Whether natural or artificial. So once again, we're starting with the land we're talking about at above and below the earth's surface. So this gets somewhat technical here, because when you're thinking of real estate, you're probably thinking, Of course, the land that you have and then basically what's constructed, what's going to be attached to it. And then there could be some debate you want to be clear on, well, how much do I have underneath there? Meaning if I get if there was oil underneath there or something like that, you know what? The rights underneath and above basically the land in terms of air space and so on as well.

So real estate is defined as land above and below the earth's surface, including all things permanently attached to it, whether natural or artificial. So for practical purposes, the term real estate can be used interchangeably with real property. So you're often going to see those basically interchangeable personal property. On the other hand, personal property is a class, a property that can include any asset other than real estate. So when we think about personal property, if you think about it just generally, you probably say, well, personal property means anything I personally own. But really, we're trying to basically kind of distinguish real property from her personal property in this context here. And notice the personal property is basically going to see everything other than the real estate property.

So we've got real estate that we've just defined as basically the land and the things attached to the land and then personal properties, everything else. And if the real estate property represents things that are attached to the land, then you would think that the personal property would be things that are not attached to the land and therefore more easily movable. One of the major definitions is difference. Differences in the types of property is the movability. Obviously, there's pros and cons of owning the land. You've got the land and the building on top of it. One of the downsides that could be that you can't, Of course, move the house too, too easily. And Of course, you can't move the land itself as well.

Personal property is going to be as things typically have lesser value, but possibly movable type of things generally. So personal property. Is a class of property that can include any assets other than real estate. The distinguishing factor between personal property and real estate or real property is that personal property is movable as opposed to being permanently attached to the land. So in other words, it isn't fixed permanently to one particular location, and it also not generally taxed like a fixed property. So we'll get into taxes later. But obviously, when you talk about the large properties, such as the home and land and so on, fixed property, you've got different property tax taxes that could be imposed on it than personal property, than movable type of property.

So then we got freehold estates. So the definition of freehold estates, freehold estates are estates of indefinite duration that can exist for a lifetime or forever. So when we're thinking about the freehold estate in terms of the owning of the real property, we're thinking about generally the real property that's going to have an ownership of a lifetime or forever. Typically, when we're thinking about a home, we might be thinking about the type of property that we have and we can basically pass on an inheritance and so on and so forth. So some types of freehold estates are classified as estates of inheritance. The states continue to be on the life of the holder and descend to their living heirs on death in accordance with will or by law.

The typical kind of home might be the way that we would generally think of a standard situation in that, you know, you own the home, you pass it on at death with a will or by law. Other freeholder states are referred to as estates, not of inheritance or life. Estates of these exist only for the term of the person's life. So it's possible then to have the freehold estate for a lifetime, but not be able to, in essence, pass it on at the point of death. The ordinary conventional life estate with remainder or revision, is an example. It does not continue for an indefinite period. Instead, it terminates when the person whose life the estate is based on or the life tenant becomes deceased. Then we have the non possession interest, the non possessory interest, the right to use or restrict the use of another person's real property or land.

And this may be the result of, say, a lease would be one of the common examples that would first come to mind. In some cases, the non possessory interest comes from a voluntary contract between two parties, like in the case of a lease agreement. So one person basically leases the use of the property to another person. Other times to not possess interest occurs because of a court order like a lean against the property. So if there's a court order that puts a lean against the property, then you could end up in this situation as well, where another person has the right to use or restrict the use of another person's real property or land. For example, a federal tax lien may be filed with the court in the county in which a delinquent taxpayers or real estate is located.

Deed

Real estate investment deed. Get ready because it's time to raise the stakes with real estate. Like with any other specialized area, real estate has its own specialized terms and definitions, terms and definitions, we need to know in order to communicate properly within the field, we're going to be looking into the definition of a deed here, noting that we're going to be referencing Investopedia so that you can look up more information with regards to terms and definitions that are investment related. So we're looking at the deed, the deed, which can be defined as a signed legal document that grants its holder ownership to an asset, but may set a number of conditions on the transfer of the title.

The deed is not a title. Instead, it is the vehicle for transferring a title. So when we're thinking about land in particular, we're thinking about real estate, things that are permanently attached to the land and things that are permanently attached to it. We can't move the land. The land is where it is. We need some way to define who has ownership, who has title to the land. That's going to have to be done with documentation and through some kind of legal process. The deed helps us to do that. It helps us to transfer the land. But the deed itself isn't a title, because there could be conditions in which people can argue or dispute the particular deed. There could be different types of deeds that will take a look at shortly.

And there could be other claims that that could be claimed against the deed, even though there's a deed that has then been transferred. Note that when you think about land, Of course, you can think about really unusual types of circumstances with regards to ownership and title over a long period of time, because obviously the land's been there for a long period of time. And you need to be able in order to determine title, to track the ownership and what has happened with regards to the changing hands of ownership over time to determine who legally has the rightful claim, the rightful title to the property. Again, the deed can help to settle some of those kinds of disputes.

So it is the deed, if the deed is not written, notarized and entered into the public record. It could be open to legal challenges and delays. So obviously, if the deed isn't written, it's going to be a lot more difficult to prove it in a legal situation if it's not notarized. Then you don't have that second verification that's going to be less insurance to it. And if it's not entered into public record, what you want is for the deed to be entered into into public record generally, because if someone else is making a claim, they're going to be making a claim based on the information that is public record. And again, the land is where the land is. So you need to basically claim that that, you know, that is your land in a public way.

Public record generally will help to sort out those types of claims that actually have ownership to it. So if those things aren't there, then it could be more likely that they're going to be open to challenges and delays. There are three main types. There's the grant deed, the warranty deed and the quitclaim deed. So let's take a look at those shortly. We got the warranty deed, a document often used in real estate that provides the greatest amount of protection to the purchaser of the property. So typically, if you're purchasing the property, you want the greatest amount of protection. So you're basically looking for generally we have a warranty deed, the deed pledges or warrants that the owner owns the property free and clear of any outstanding liens, mortgages or other encumbrances, other problems on the property that could cause you some, you know, people to make claims against you.

Once you are the owner of the property. So things, Of course, that could cause problems. If there were, you know, Lean's on the property, mortgages and so on, so on, as you took ownership of the property. So the grantor is responsible for a breach of any warranties and guarantees, therefore placing a great amount of risk on the grantor. So note the guarantor, then the one that's going to be taken on, in essence, the responsibility in that case to give the purchaser here the greatest, you know, support as they have the warranty deed that they have, you know, for claim to the property clean and free. So it's a document often used in real estate that provides the greatest amount of protection to the purchaser of the property. It pledges or warrants that the owner owns the property free and clear of any outstanding liens of mortgages or other encumbrances.

We then have these special warranty deeds, a special warranty deed as a deed in which the seller of a piece of property only warrants against problems or encumbrances in the property title that occurred during his ownership. So notice the lowering of the bar here. So it's a little bit lower here. So if you're the purchaser and you're purchasing it from someone else, then someone else is saying, hey, you know, you know this I'm I'm it's free from anything during the time period that I had it. But obviously, the property is quite old because it's land. You know, it could have a. History beyond that.

So it's possible that you could have claims that would basically go on beyond the ownership, Of course, of the prior individual that you are purchasing from. So once again, a special warranty deed is a deed in which the seller of a piece of property only warrants against problems or encumbrances in the property title that occurred during his ownership of the property. So if there's a problem prior to that, that didn't really come up during his ownership or, you know, it's a prior claim or something like that, that's where there still could be an essence of the problem. And obviously, you could think of different circumstances where this may be, well, you know, higher or lesser assurance, obviously, if they owned the property for a year, that would, you know, would be a less assurance than if they own the property for the last 50 years or something like that, then you would think they might have a bigger claim. But in any case, a special warranty deed guarantees two things.

The grantor owns and can and can sell the property and the property incurred no encumbrances during his ownership. The special warranty deed is more limited than the more common general warranty deed, which covers the entire history of the property. Then we have a trustee, which is a little bit different. It's basically a trust. You can see the trust which indicates that a third party could be involved. So in financial real estate transaction trust, deeds transfer the legal title of a property to a third party. So there's that third party in the trust component of the trust deed, such as a bank escrow company or title company to hold until the borrower repays the debt to the lender. Trust deeds are used in place of mortgages in several states. So this could be dependent on the state that you are.

We might talk more about this scenario in future chapters. Lastly, we have the quitclaim deed. A quitclaim deed releases a person's interest in a property without state in the nature of the person's interest or rights, and with no warranties of that person's interest or rights in the property. A quick claim deed makes no assurance that the grantor actually has an ownership interest in a property. It merely states that if the grantor does, they release those ownership rights.

So it's just going to be the releasing of the rights that are quittin of the claim. In essence, when might you be using this? Quitclaim deeds are typically used to transfer property and non sale situations, such as transfer of property between family members. So if a sale if it's a sale type of situation, you would think a higher level of deed, a higher level of assurance would be necessary. If it's between family members and a non sale type of transaction, it might be easier just to have the quitclaim and it may put less obligation on the person that's giving the property from one family member to the other.

Title Insurance

Real estate investment, title insurance. Get ready because it's time to raise the stakes with real estate. Like with any other specialized area, real estate has its own specialized terms and definitions, which we need to understand in order to properly communicate within the field. We're going to be looking at this time at title insurance, noting that when we're looking at terms and definitions, what the referencing Investopedia, which is a place you can go to, to look at terms and definitions for investment related items, title insurance is going to be a key component with most real estate transactions, one which we need to understand what is happening and how it's going to be fitting in within the process.

So title insurance can be defined as a form of indemnity insurance that protects lenders and home buyers from financial loss due to defects in a title to a property. So obviously, generally in general, we got a seller that's going to be selling to the buyer. The title then transfers from the seller to the buyer. What if, however, there's problems with the title, the claim to the title? Then who's going to be responsible for that? And can we get some assurance or some coverage in the event that there is some kind of problem? And the title insurance is going to fit. And this is where the title insurance in essence, fits in.

So the most common type of title insurance is the lender's title insurance. Lender's title insurance is something the borrower purchases to protect the lender. So the borrower. So we're talking typically about the purchaser here that is going to be borrowing and they're going to need this lender's title insurance in order to protect the lender. The person that's making the loan, the other type is the owner's title. Insurance owner's title insurance is often paid by the seller to protect the buyer's equity in the property. So notice, if you're the seller, we're saying you're the person that's basically saying, I have claim to this property, I'm selling it to you in order and for money. So there's basically if you get the title insurance, you're basically saying, in good faith, I have I have the ownership.

You know, it's a way of assuring that you have the ownership. So typically it's going to be falling on the seller then. In other words, once again, owner's title insurance is often paid by the seller to protect the buyer's equity in the property. So indemnity insurance, just what is indemnity insurance? Notice up here, we said that the title insurance is a form of indemnity insurance. So just indemnity insurance in general is a type of insurance policy where the insurance company guarantees compensation for losses or damages sustained by a policyholder. And dignity insurance is designed to protect professionals and businesses, business owners, when they are found to be at fault for a specific event like misjudgment. Certain professionals must carry indemnity insurance, for example, those involved in financial and legal services, like as financial advisers, insurance agents, accountants, mortgage brokers and attorneys.

So you may be aware of indemnity insurance in general, medical malpractice and errors and omissions insurance are also examples of indemnity insurance. OK, bad title. So we need to know what a bad title is. In essence, this is one thing that the insurance possibly could be protecting against. So what is a bad title? A legal document associated with an asset that does not grant ownership to the entity that holds the title. So there's going to be a problem with the transfer of the ownership. When we have this issue of the bad title, they could be the result of legal issues, financial problems, or even simple clerical errors. They are almost always associated with real estate and can stop the title holder from selling the property.

So obviously, this could cause a problem within the transaction when we're looking at the transaction between the sale of real real estate. There's a lot of components that are going to be involved. And, you know, a bad title is going to be a component that could, you know, stop the process. So clear or perfect. Titles are necessary to legally transfer a piece of property. A title holder can clear up a title by resolving the legal, financial or clerical issues. So if there is a bad title, the question is, can you clear it up? And then, you know, continue on with the process. Title insurance.

So title insurance protects lenders and buyers from financial loss due to defects in a title to a property. So if there's a problem with the title and the property, then as we go through the transfer process, that's what the title insurance can basically help with to make sure that you have the actual claim, you know, to the property if there's any problem with it. Then again, who's going to be a liability liable for those kinds of problems? So the most common claims filed against a title are back to. Axis leans and conflicting will so back taxes Lean's conflicting wills. The one time fee paid for title insurance covers up pricey administration fees for in-depth searches of title data to protect against claims for past occurrences.

So in other words, if you didn't have the title insurance, then how would you really be sure that there aren't these kinds of problems with relation to the transfer of the title? How would you know it was a clear transfer? Well, then you might have to pay for basically an in-depth search to double check because you don't totally trust, Of course, the person that's selling the property, you don't know them. So you'd have to basically pay someone to do an in-depth search. That would be a long, costly process. So the title insurance then is generally going to be the party that will be taken to doing that kind of process and pain and basically earning in an insurance format for that process.

So that's kind of where they fit in. So any real estate transaction needs to have a clear title to insure the property is free from Ilene's. So when the transfer happens, you want it to be clear. It has to be clear so that, you know, you know, what exactly is going on with this kind of large transaction. So a title insurance policy will cover many risks like flood records, incorrect ownership and falsified documents. Clear title. So what is the clear title? Remember, we need a clear title in order to facilitate the transaction for the real estate transaction. A clear title is needed for any real estate transaction. Title companies must do a search on every title to check for claims or liens of any kind of any kind against them before they can issue. So you have to have a clear title so that there aren't any problems so that you can go through the process.

So one more time, the title companies must do a search on every title to check the claims or liens of any kind against them before they can be issued. So title search and examination of public records to determine and confirm a property's legal ownership. So when you think about the actual time title SURP search, you want to think about, OK, who has ownership to this? Once again, it can be quite complex in some instances if there's some ambiguity in terms of the recording of the documentation and the public record that's going back. So hopefully you can look at the public record and it will be a fairly clear type of process. And you can determine the chain of ownership going forward and then and then move from there.

So once again, the title Search and examination of public records to determine and confirm a property's legal ownership. It helps check whether there are any claims on the property. Erroneous surveys and unresolved building code violations are two examples of blemishes that can make the title, quote, dirty title and quote, title insurance title insurance protects lenders as well as home buyers against loss or damage that happen from liens, encumbrances or defects in a property's title or actual ownership. Common claims filed against a title are back taxes, Lean's from mortgage loans, home equity lines of credit, or the easements and conflicting wills.

Traditional insurance generally protects against future events, whereas the title insurance protects against claims from past occurrences. In other words, that's one of the differences between title insurance and general insurance. If you pay for normal insurance, like car insurance or something, you're paying against the possibility of a future problem happening. When you're looking at the title insurance, you're still kind of paying for something that could cause a future problem. The future arises in, you know, the problem happens in the future, but it's caused by some claim that was in the past, because generally it would be a claim before, you know, the transfer happened or something like that, which is kind of distinctive of the title insurance.

So the basic owner's basic title insurance policy usually covers the following hazards owned by another party. Incorrect signatures on document forgery and fought fraud, fraud records, restrictive covenants, terms that reduce the value or enjoyment like unrecorded easements, encumbrances or judgments against property like outstanding lawsuits and lean's so types of title insurance. Then there are two types of title insurance that we need to kind of have an idea of both of them. There's the lender's title insurance and there's the owner's title. IT insurance included extended policies. Just about all lenders require the borrower. So the buyer that's going to have the loan, the borrower to protect the lender's title insurance policy, which protects the lender to the event.

The seller was not legally able to transfer the title of ownership rights. A lender's policy only protects the lender against lost and issued policies and issued policy signifies the. Completion of a title search offering some assurance to the buyer because title searches are not infallible and the owner remains at risk of financial loss. There is a need for additional protection in the form of the owner's title insurance policy. In other words, you're going to have the title search happening, but they're not infallible. They might not catch something. And if something happens at a later point in time, then the owner may then be responsible and the title insurance might help in that situation. So you will typically then have the owner's title insurance. So owner's title insurance, which is generally purchased by the seller.

So its purchase generally by the seller here to protect the buyer against defects in the title is optional. So once again, on the owner's title insurance side of things, you're saying if the person that is selling it, the person that is selling is saying I'm the one that's selling. And so possibly in a way to guarantee that it's a clear, you know, title. They're the ones that are generally going to be paying for the owner's title insurance, which will help them, once they have the property against future claims. That could happen basically against the property that might have gotten through, in essence, or not be picked up during the sales transaction with the title search. So purchasing title insurance and escrow or closing agent initiates the insurance process at completion of the property purchase agreement.

There are four major U.S. title insurance underwriters. That's the Fidelity National Financial First American title insurance company, Old Republic National Title Insurance Company and Stewart Title Guaranty Company. There are also regional title insurance companies to choose from as well. Purchasing title insurance. The cost of owner's title insurance is dependent on the state you live in and the insurance provider you choose and the purchase price of your home. A lender's policy and owner's policy are often required together to guarantee everyone is protected at closing. The parties will purchase title insurance for one.

So for a one time fee, the Real Estate Settlement Procedures Act RSPCA prohibits celibates sellers from requiring purchase from a specific title insurance carrier to protect abuse from happening. So risk of not having title insurance, so what if you don't get title insurance, what if you don't have it? I know no. Title insurance exposes Treant transacting parties to significant risk if a title defect is present. So if there's a problem in the title, Of course, then that would be more problematic if you don't have the title insured. So, for example, imagine a homebuyer after closing finds out about unpaid property taxes from the prior owner. So now you own the property. There's unpaid property taxes against the property that you weren't aware of.

And now and now basically, you would generally. You know what? Who is going to be responsible for that? So with no title insurance, the financial burden of this claim for back taxes falls solely with the buyer. They will have to either pay the outstanding property taxes or risk losing the home to the tax, to the taxing entity risk of not having it. On the other hand, with title insurance, the coverage protects the buyer for as long as they own or have an interest in the property in a similar way. The lender's title insurance covers banks and other mortgage lenders from an unrecorded liens, unrecorded access rights and other defects in case of a borrower default. If there are any issues with the property title, a lender would be covered up to the amount of the mortgage.

Real Estate Documents Needing to Be Recorded

Real estate investment, real estate documents needing to be recorded, get ready because it's time to raise the stakes with real estate. Real estate documents needing to be recorded, referencing Investopedia, where you can go for more information, as in any transaction, keeping an official paper trail and a record of any sale or change in ownership is an important part of verifying the history of a given property or a purchase. So obviously, this documentation is quite important when we're talking about real estate being actual land in the things that are going to be attached to the land, because those things are not going to be movable. And therefore, the only way we're going to have any idea of that claim to them is with the documentation, some type of formal documentation, hopefully, of the public record to help us with that.

So recording can be defined as the act of putting a document into the official county records. So what's it into the official county records? And then we have that public record which can't help us to sort out the claims for the property. So recording is an important process that provides a traceable chain of title to a property. So obviously, if we're looking at the recording, what we would like to see is this nice traceable trail of the property going from point to point so that we can see where the ownership is taking place. Not always is it so nice and neat of a traceable trail, but that's going to be the idea so that we can sort out any disputes.

There are more than 100 types of documents that can be recorded depending on the type of property and type of real estate transaction. The most common documents are related to mortgages, deeds, easements, foreclosures, estoppel leases, licenses and fees. Some of the most important real estate documents list ownership, encumbrances and leane property. These documents are used to maintain proper real estate transactions. So real estate documents needed to be recorded. Recorded is the act of putting a document into official county records, especially for real estate and property transactions. That provides a traceable chain of title recorded documents that do not establish who owns a property.

Instead, these public records are used to help resolve disputes between parties with competing claims to a property. So you're going to look at the recorded records, the recorded records, any one recorded record in and of itself. Does it necessarily say that that is the title or the claim to it? If given a record, that should make it easier to sort out who has claims to the property through the traceability of the records, which then can be reviewed. And then you could go from there in terms of determining who has title or who has claim to understand which documents have been or must be recorded.

Check with your state and county recording division recording systems that vary by state and are established by individual state statutes. So the idea of recording the documentation to have that trail of title or the documentations and claims to it will be the same. But the actual process of the recording could vary from state to state. So you want to check out where you are located with regards to what the process will look like. Not all states use a process of instrument recording to track titles. Some states use land restriction systems. Instead, it is the responsibility of their local, county or state to make sure that these official documents are kept on file. Recorded documents do not establish who owns a property, establishing who owns a property is the function of a title that establishes the legal owner of the asset. Recorded documents are made public to be used to help resolve disputes between parties with competing claims to a property.

So obviously, again, they got those competing claims. Then the public records can help in that dispute and resolve those disputes. For example, if two different claimants have conflicting deeds to a property, the date of the recording can be used to determine the ownership timeline. So if you see these two deeds that are going to be involved, then the question is, OK, well, how are we going to dispute this? If you have two different people that have these two deeds they're claiming here, then possibly you can take a look at the dates of the deeds and take a look at the timeline.

And in most cases, these public records provide clarity. Usually the owner with the most recent deed would be considered the rightful owner real estate recording systems with mortgage liens. Courts use the date of a recording to determine the priority for which Lean's should receive payments first to understand which documents have been or must be recorded. Check with your state and county recording division. Some states have also passed recording acts, which are statutes that establish how official records are kept recording, and provide information for both government authorities and for buyers and sellers of real estate property.

Property Rights Limitations

Real estate investment, property rights and limitations. Get ready because it's time to raise the stakes with real estate. Like with any other specialized area, real estate has its own specialized terms and definitions, which we need to understand in order to communicate properly within the field will be continued on learning some specialized terms and definitions here, referencing Investopedia, which is a place you can go to look up terms and definitions that are investment related. Getting more detail on them. The terms that we're looking at here are going to be terms that are going to be related to restrictions we would have on the properties. So in other words, if we own real estate, the general idea is that we can do what we want with the property that we own, unless there's some type of government restrictions stopping us from doing something on the property.

Now, note that these restrictions can kind of go both ways in terms of are they beneficial or harmful to us when we first hear them. We think the restrictions are bad because you're restricting me from doing something with my property, which is true if it's going to be a restriction from what you want to do. So if I wanted to build up on my property, for example, and they put some kind of restriction that I can't build above a certain level, then and I want to do that, that would be a restriction for us. However, they can also be kind of beneficial to the value of the property.

If there are restrictions on other people, meaning, for example, if I've already built my home and I'm happy with it, and then there's the restriction on other people building up higher or restriction on other people building at all, that then restricts the the supply of the properties around the area, and it could actually lead to an increase in the value of the property. So in that case, if you're the homeowner, it's kind of like you climbed up the pole already and then you greased the pole so no one else can climb up on it through zoning restrictions. Right. So there could be a kind of a double edged sword on the on the zoning restrictions as to whether or not they'd be bad for a particular homeowner in a particular area or good to a particular homeowner, or how they would feel good or bad to someone else that's trying to get into the market and that particular area.

So keeping that in mind first will be taking a look at zoning. So zoning, municipal or local laws or regulations that govern how real property can and cannot be used in certain geographic areas. So they're going to be mapping out the geographic area. They're going to put some regulations in terms of what you can and cannot do within that mapped out area. So, for example, zoning laws can limit commercial or industrial use of land to prevent oil, manufacturing or other types of businesses from building in residential neighborhoods. So note, obviously, when you're thinking about purchasing property, you've got to make sure that what you want to do with the property will be permitted within the laws that are going to be taking place.

And you might also have to predict what you think's going to happen, you know, in the future with regards to the zoning type laws as well. Now, obviously, when you think about these types of restrictions, when you have a residential property, no one really likes someone to move in like an oil manufacturing company next to you or any industrial business right next door or something like that. So you can think about, obviously, the people that already own the buildings or residential areas then would have an incentive to restrict business, especially manufacturing business that would be built next door to them, because that would be beneficial, you would think, to their property value. Once they're there.

So so again, you can kind of but it would also you can kind of see the pros and cons that would be with these kind of zoning laws and the incentives people would have, whether they're trying to go in or move into a community or whether they're already living in a community, how they might, you know, view these kind of zoning laws so zoning laws can be modified or suspended if the construction of a property will serve to help the community advanced economically. The zoning allows local governments to regulate which areas under their jurisdiction may have real estate or land use for a particular purpose. So they're going to basically restrict, you know, how the land or the building would be used.

Examples of ALONI zoning classifications include residential, commercial, agricultural, industrial or hotel hospitality, as well as other more specific designations. So we can imagine basically mapping out here, having these classifications about the basic zoning rules and those categories. A residential commercial, agricultural, industrial hotel, hospitality and possibly more specific in certain circumstances, they can be changed by a local government as long as they fall within the state and federal statutes. So obviously, you know, there's something that can change. You can change the zoning, but then it would be a government kind of process in order to do so. A particular plot of land can be rezoned based on consideration.

So how zoning works, zoning outlines. What type of developer? And operational use of land is allowed on a given tract, municipalities generally partitioned districts, neighborhoods according to a master plan, and then it may be done to promote economic development, control the flow of traffic, manage noise levels, reserve living space for residents, and protect certain resources. So, again, why might these be done? You can see how, you know, we basically map these things out. They're basically going to say this is what is allowed in particular areas. Why might that be done? It's important to kind of understand why these things could be done again from someone who's going to move into the area.

If you're trying to purchase within the area, what's going to be your reason for purchasing in the area, and then also have the perspective of someone that already lives in the area. What might be their perspective in terms of the zoning laws and what they would want to go for. As you think of zoning as a government thing, which is going to be, you know, done by elections and whatnot. So it may be done to promote economic development. So obviously that people that are in the particular area may be happy for certain types of economic development and may not like some other type of business development.

Right. If you're actually living in the area, control the flow of traffic. So obviously, you know, if you're living in an area, you want the traffic to flow, but you don't want the freeway, you know, right next to you or something like that. And so you could see where the incentives would be for people that are involved in the decision making process, for a government kind of action, to manage noise levels. So, again, you could see where that would be in terms of if you already live in a neighborhood versus if you're moving into a neighborhood versus, you know, if you're a business type of business that's moving into the neighborhood, what your incentives might be for these different things.

Reserve living space for residents and protect certain resources. Now, this last one is obviously one, protecting certain resources. That's the classical example of some of you know, once you already have a home and you're living in the home, you've already climbed up the pole and then you greased the pole. Right. You say, hey, if you start, if you build any more houses around here, then you're going to, you know, you're going to, you know, endanger an endangered butterfly or something like that. And that could restrict the building around you, which obviously increases the property value of the people that already have built in the area.

So you can see how these laws have an impact on the property value. The more restrictions to building actually the higher and more inflated the prices of the homes will generally be. So how zoning works, a local government could ban the use of residential property for business purposes to keep commercial activity confined to specific parts of town. Zoning can lead to conflicts if residents dispute the designated usage. Zoning laws can also regulate the details of construction in specific neighborhoods. For example, zoning can limit the maximum height of buildings in a given area, regardless of the type of construction allowed.

So the height is another area that is often under controversy because there's often view kind of kind of controversies, meaning if you have a house on the whole, on a hill and you have a nice view of a landscape or a view of the beach, and then someone right underneath you of the hill builds a house that's higher, and then it will it will get in the way of your vehicle to to some extent. Then you can see again where the incentives happen with the zoning laws to try to restrict people from building up in those instances as well. And, you know, restricting people from building up, for example, there's many places that say, you know, they've restricted building up.

And if you can't build up, meaning then you can't build living facilities. As for as many people, because you're restricted, you know, you only have so much space at some point you start building up. And so that, again, is another way that that can restrict the amount of people that would be in a particular area and that would probably lead to increase in the prices of the residents that are already in the area. So high rise residents or offices may be banned on particular parcels through zoning, regardless of whether the building otherwise comply with the laws.

So how zoning works, continued zoning restrictions will generally influence prices when purchasing a piece of property. So, again, you got to kind of have an idea of what the zoning restrictions are and what might be the zoning restrictions going forward, because they're one of the really big factors in the long term as to what the property value is going to do. Is the property value going to go up or down? And it's kind of a funny thing that the more restrictions there are for other people, again, it's kind of like grease in the pool once you've already climbed up it, that that would mean that the housing prices would probably go up. And you could see this if you look at the expensive areas on the maps for.

Our homes, you could see, it's probably highly correlated and completely related to how many zoning restrictions they've put in place as well. So real estate might sell at a premium based on how many limits were put in a place by the municipality. So then we have the eminent domain. So eminent domain is the next thing, which is a government imposed kind of thing that can they can impinge on your property rights, because once again, you would think that the general idea, if it's your property, you can do, in essence, what you want to do, as long as you're not disturbing other people and their ability to do what they want to do, unless there's going to be a restrictions and eminent domain domain is the other big one that that there's a lot of dispute about. So the right of governments like the United States to usurp private property for public use following fair compensation.

So in other words, they say, hey, we're coming in, we're taking your property, and you say, hey, this is my property. I have to write the property. That's one of the rights I have. Right. And they said, no, not in this instance, because we have eminent domain in this certain situation. So it's a very touchy thing in terms of individual rights in the United States. The idea is, you know, how much you know, what right do they have to take your property and what would be considered fair compensation? And basically, if eminent domain comes in and they declare that they're going to take your property. Then there's situations where the property value actually goes down, Of course, because everybody knows that the government wants to move in and take their property.

And by the time they actually do it, the housing market prices obviously go down because everybody knows that they've declared it to be a property that's going to be taken over and whatnot. And then by the time they get paid out, the property level could be lower. So there's a lot of interesting issues with regards to property rights and eminent domain. But obviously, if it's an area that is in danger of being declared an eminent domain, then you've got to be aware of that. Of course, all things from aerospace land and contract rights to intellectual property is subject to eminent domain if a case can be made for its public use. So the idea being if the public will benefit the public is going to benefit from the eminent domain over and above the benefit of this one individual.

And we can't, you know, sacrifice the public good for this one piece of property and therefore, the government is going to do what they want to do. The classical example would be like we're building a freeway through here or something like that, which is a public good that's going to be benefiting everyone. Or the classic example was the train, you know, in the trains going through and whatnot. We're trying to rule the track here. And you got you know, it's got to go where it's got to go. But now they've kind of increased it to other types of things, actually increasing it and then giving rights to private entrepreneurs or private construction and whatnot in areas which become more controversial.

So the legal debates around unfair and invoking eminent domain, like when property owners are not fairly compensated, it's called inverse condemnation. Eminent domain, eminent domain is a right granted under the Fifth Amenta Amendment of the Constitution. Similar powers can be found in most common law nations under different names. So in the United States, you have eminent domain. It's a similar kind of concept in other areas as well. It might be under different names. Private property is taken through condemnation proceedings. Owners can challenge that the Galatea of the seizure and settle the matter of fair market value are used for compensation.

So you can't obviously try to argue the legality of the seizure that it's done in accordance with the law. And then you can argue, Of course, whether the compensation is appropriate as well. The most straightforward example of condemnation involves land and buildings seized to make way for public projects. So if you have a public project, like a freeway, like a train, that would be the most common kind of example, the most clear cut example. They're saying, hey, look, we've got to put this this train needs to be connected in the entire United States or so on. So, you know, it's for the public good to put it through this particular area. It may include aerospace, water, dirt, timber and rock appropriation from private land for the construction of roads. Eminent domains can include leases, stocks and investment funds.

Promissory Notes Provisions

Real estate investment, promissory notes provision. Get ready because it's time to raise the stakes with real estate. Now we're going to take a look at the components of a promissory note when we're dealing with real estate. Usually we will have a note or loan related to it. So we want to look at the components of the notes and the loans at this time in future chapters. We'll zoom in on certain components of the loans, including doing calculations such as that calculation of the payments that change on the calculation of the payment that could take place with different interest rates and the creation of amortization tables and all that kind of good stuff here. We want to look at the major components. We will be dealing with some more definitions here.

When thinking about definitions, we're going to reference Investopedia, which is a place you can go if you have investment related terms for more detail about investment related terms. So we have the promissory notes provisions. A promissory note has a lot of components and pieces to it. So some of these components and pieces, Of course, are going to be used for the calculations of things like payments. And some of them are going to be having to do with what's going to happen with regards to the promissory note, given certain conditions or future activities that happen in the future. So obviously, we have the amount borrowed. Typically when dealing with a real estate transaction, you're going to have to put some amount down.

We might then borrow the rest of it, using the rest of it to complete the purchasing process then the amount that it's going to be needed. The purchasing power of that to purchase the home or whatever real estate we are purchasing. We have the rate of interest. Obviously, the rate of interest is in essence, going to be the cost of us using the purchasing power in order to purchase whatever real estate that we are purchasing. You can think of interest as similar to rent, meaning if you were to rent something like an apartment or something like that, you are paying for the use of the apartment when you're looking at a loan. They're giving you something.

They're giving you purchasing power that you don't currently have and you're going to be giving it back in the future. That's basically a similar kind of process. You're paying for the rent of the purchasing power, which is in essence the interest that will be paid dollar amount and the due dates and the number of payments. These are going to be components. And these will generally be components that are going to be necessary for us to kind of calculate what the actual loan payments will be and so on and so forth. So we'll deal with them more in future chapters when we start to break down the loan calculation. So obviously, we need the dollar amounts, the due dates and the number of payments that are going to be involved. The maturity date.

So how far out in the future will it mature? The reference to the security for the loan. So note again, these top items up here, the amount borrowed, the interest rate, that dollar amount due dates and the number of payments and the maturity date, these are the general components we will put together when we do the calculations of the payments and so on. How much interest is going to be paid per year. And this amortization table, then we have, Of course, items that aren't really related to those calculation numbers, but are crucial to the loan itself, Of course. And that's a reference to the security on the loan.

So security is something that's going to support the loan. And that usually, Of course, will give the lender more security about the loan being repaid. The security for real estate will typically be the real estate that is going to be purchased, and therefore they have reBook in the event that the loan is not going to be repaid. That's usually beneficial to the institution to lower the risk, and that's usually beneficial to the borrower to lower the risk, because then they might get better terms, better interest rates for it. So defaults will talk maybe a little bit more about that in a future chapter here. But what is going to happen if there's a default on the loan so payments aren't being made or something like that? So security for the loan.

So remember, when you're dealing with a loan that is for real estate, then generally you're talking about a larger dollar amount. The institution is going to want more security, lowering the risk on their side in order to be able to offer the best terms for the borrower. And that usually will result in the security of the real estate itself. So security in general will be a security interest on a loan is a legal claim on collateral that the borrower provides that allows the lender to repossess the collateral and sell it if the loan goes bad. So clearly, real estate is a really good thing in terms of the bank's perspective to have as collateral generally, because usually the real estate value is fairly stable and or increases in normal times.

And even if it goes down, if there's a substantial down payment, then they should be OK in the event that there's a problem. And you know, what would happen is they could basically, if their payments didn't happen and they repossessed the home, they can generally sell the home and then recover the loan balance to that that was secured. So that would be the idea. Obviously, that would lower the risk. Or the bank or the institution giving the loan, which would allow them to offer better deals for the low and lower rates and so on. So a security interest lowers the risk to the lender, allowing it to charge lower interest rates on the loan. Lower interest means that the borrower's cost of capital will also be reduced. So it can be a good thing for both sides to default.

So the term default happens when a borrower is unable to make timely payments, misses payments or avoids or stops making payments on interest or principal owed. So clearly, if you're the lender, that's what you don't want to have happen, because you're making your money by giving the loan, by getting the money back. Just like if you were renting out an apartment or something, you want the apartment back at the end, plus you want the rent on it, which Of course, is basically the interest. So defaults can happen. Unsecured debt, like a mortgage loan secured by a house or unsecured debt like credit cards or student loans. So a default just can be in general if you took out a loan, no matter what type of loan, different types of loan, whether it be secured or not, if it was not secured, then the lender doesn't have as much reBook.

They have less, you know, a capacity to collect on it if it was secured than they have that reBook, Of course. Defaults can have consequences, like lowering credit scores reduces the chance of obtaining credit in the future and raising interest rates on existing debt as well as any new obligations. So in the event that there was a default, then that even if you might say, well, then I can lose the property, but obviously there could be other consequences beyond that as well, including the credit score going down, making it more difficult to get financing in the future and so on.

So promissory note provisions, continued penalties for late payments and forbearance provisions. So what kind of penalties would be involved for future kinds of events that are violations of the loan terms provision for EDG unscheduled or early payments? Now, this is something that's often you want to make sure that you have an idea of what the loan amount is here, because notice you're usually looking at longer term loans if you take a 30 year loan out. Then the question is, you know, you're paying interest for 30 years. From the bank's perspective, there's kind of a double edged sword. Right. If they get paid back sooner.

They would like that to some degree because they would be paid, because that would be less risky. But on the other hand, they're also losing interest. The longer the loan is out, then the more they're going to earn over the loan term in terms of interest. So what you would like to do as the person who is taking out the loan is have the capacity to pay off the loan earlier, if we would like. So, in other words, if we can have the security of having a 30 year loan, even though we plan on paying off the loan in 15 years, then that could give us some more leeway to in the event that we have problems, pay off the lower amount of the loan because it's a 30 year loan which would lower the payments, but also be able to pay the loan off early.

If we choose to do so, if we can do so, which would lower the interest over the full term of the loan, because we'd be paying off sooner. Maybe it'd be like renting the apartment for a lesser period of time, and therefore we'd be paying less rent on it, which in this case would be of interest in that case. So you want to make sure that you have the capacity typically to pay off the loan earlier, if you can. Usually that would be beneficial to have that flexibility as the borrower. Notification of default. An acceleration clause. Non ReBook clause in the event there is a non reBook clause.

Loans are generally with reBook if the bad boy provisions are violated. This could include fraud or chapter. Another example would be if the borrower willfully damages the asset, the borrower will generally be held personally responsible for the damage. So in other words, clearly, if you were to leave the home, if someone was to say we're going to default on the home or something like that, and then the person destroys the property that they're leaving out of anger and so on. Then are they responsible for the reduction in the value of the property that they cause on the way out, in essence? So the promissory note provisions, continued loan assumption ability.

We'll talk about the future here and future advances. We'll talk a little bit more about it here. So loans assume ability, assumable mortgage, an arrangement where an outstanding mortgage and its terms can be transferred from the current owner to a buyer when interest rates rise. An assumable mortgage is attractive to a buyer who can take on an existing loan with a lower rate. So if they can basically assume the loan and you have higher rates and basically the current loan was created with a lower rate, then that could be attractive. You, a buyer, USDA, FHA and V.A.

Loans are assumed when certain conditions are met, and then we have future advances, a clause in a mortgage that provides for additional availability of funds under the loan contract, meaning you could basically take more money out in the future, possibly if you had a clause of future advances, possibly in the loan. If a future advance clause is included in a loan contract, then the borrower can rely on obtaining funds from the lender under the terms of the contract without being required to obtain another loan for additional funds. Future advance clauses may or may not have certain contingencies that make the borrower eligible for future advances.

Mortgage Instrument

Real estate investment, mortgage instrument. Get ready because it's time to raise the stakes with real estate. Like with any other specialized area, real estate has its own specialized terms and definitions, which we will continue on focusing on here, referencing Investopedia, which is a place you can go to look up terms and definitions that are investment related and further your research there. We're focusing on the mortgage here in a prime prior chapter. We took a look at the promissory note. So we're looking at the notes and mortgages focusing on the mortgage. The note and the mortgage are not the same thing.

So generally, when we think about, say, a home purchase or real estate, we think about the note and the mortgage being kind of packaged together, which is OK, but technically they're not the same thing. The note is an obligation to pay. In essence, the loan while the mortgage pledge is the property as security. So you have the loan and then you have the pledging of the property as the security, in essence, the real estate supporting the loan, giving the lender then more security, which could influence the loan terms that would be involved, possibly lowering the interest rate lower than it otherwise would have been due to the lower risk. So the mortgagor is the borrower, the mortgagee is the lender.

This can be a little bit confusing, because when we think about a loan, we think about the lender as in essence, if it's the bank of the bank doing the lending and then the lender being the person that's getting the loan, that's going to be basically the borrower. It's when you think about the mortgage, however, notice you're the owner. If you're if you own the property, then you're saying, I own the property and I'm mortgaging it. So you are the mortgage or to the lender who is then going to be the mortgagee? Who is going to be the recipient of the mortgage in that case? So it's a kind of reverse that you might typically think of, because when you think about, again, the loan, then the lender is going to be the bank and the lender would be then the person that is taking out the loan.

So this is often confused by people who are new to the industry, minimum mortgage requirements, identification of the mortgage order and the mortgages. So obviously, we've got a list of who is who for the minimum mortgage requirements, description of the property serving as security for the loan. So clearly, if we're putting the loan on or some property as collateral, we need to be specific about what that property is, covenants and session and warranty. We'll take a look at that in a little bit more detail soon. Provision for release of dower rights. We'll take a look at that in a little bit more detail soon. Any other desired covenants and contractual agreements? So the covenant of session.

So means possession and the grantor warrants that they own the property and have the legal right to convey it. The Delaware rights, white rights, a real estate interest intended to protect a spouse who does not hold title. So to protect a spouse that does not hold title. Idaho. Arkansas. Kentucky are the only states that retain daughter rights. Dauer whites generally become effective after someone dies. Dauer rights law entitles a surviving spouse to at least one third of the deceased spouse's real property after they die. So that may or may not be then applicable to you. The important mortgage covenants, so important mortgage covenants include and will go into some of these in more detail in future chapters. So we'll go over them a little bit more quickly here.

Funds for private mortgage insurance charges and Lean's hazard insurance preservation and maintenance of the property. Breach of contracts, transfer of property or a beneficial interest. And the borrower due on sale clause continued here. Borrower's rights to reinstate a right of entry lender in possession future advances subordination clause. So we'll go into some of those in a bit more detail. So the private mortgage insurance. And we go into this in a little bit more detail in another chapter as well. But the private mortgage insurance and insurance policy that protects a lender or title holder, if the borrower defaults on the payments, passes away, or is otherwise unable to meet the contractual obligations of the mortgage.

Three types of mortgage insurance include private mortgage insurance, qualified mortgage insurance premium and mortgage title insurance. It should not be confused with the mortgage life insurance, which pertains to the protection of heirs if the borrower dies while owing mortgage payments. Then we have the mortgage lien and mortgage lean is a legal right. The lender has to take property if you fail to pay your debt. So in essence, we're talking about the mortgage here, Darlene. Then you're failing to pay the debt, allowing then possibly the property to be taken in order to settle the debt. So once again, a mortgage lead is a legal right. The lender has to take your. Property if you fail to pay your debt.

Most people mix mortgages with the actual loans made to purchase the real estate. However, a mortgage is not simply a loan. So, again, there's kind of that difference between the loan itself and the mortgage. They're kind of tied together. They're linked in some ways, but they serve, you know, the two different functions within this process. So instead, it is an interest in the real property held by the lender. The lean holder as protection in case the borrower fails to pay back the loan. So that's what the mortgage component does, preservation and maintenance of property. So we'll take a look at this in a little bit more detail. Might look something like this. Borrower shall keep the property in good repair and shall not commit waste or or permit impairment or deterioration of the property.

And she'll comply with the provisions of any lease. If this deed of trust is on a leasehold. So, in other words, you might have a condition, a clause in there to say, hey, you got to keep up the property, because if you're put in the property there as collateral, then it should be basically preservation and in good condition could be something that you as the borrower, as the lender would want to make sure is a condition so that in the event that there's going to be nonpayment, that that if you have to repossess the property, the property is of value. That should, Of course, at least cover the loan. So the borrower shall perform all of the borrower's obligations under any declaration's covenants, bylaws, rules or other documents governing the use. Ownership or occupancy of the property.

So then we have the do on sale clause, which could looks something like this mortgage or shall not sell, convey or otherwise transfer any interest in the premises, whether voluntarily or by operation of law, or agreed to do so without mortgages, prior written consent, including a any sale conveyance incumbrance assignment or other transfer of including installment land sale contracts, or the grant of a security interest in all or part of the legal or equitable title to the premises, except as otherwise permitted hereunder. So I won't go into that. And a little bit more detail. You can look at that in a little bit more detail here, but you can see why that would be important to the lender at Hazard Insurance.

So Hazard Insurance protects a property owner against damage caused by fires, severe storms and other natural disasters. This could be important, Of course, in certain circumstances, because, Of course, once again, no lender, if they're going to fall back on being able to pick up the property in the event that there was a default on the payment, the payments were not made. They want to make sure that the property has value, that they'll be able to get the claim of the value on it. And so if the property is in danger in some way, this could be important. So it usually refers to a chapter of a general homeowner's insurance policy that protects the structure of the home mortgage. The lenders often require you to have homeowners insurance to get hazard coverage in areas prone to certain risks, such as floods or land chapters.

Homeowners often opt to take out separate or additional hazard insurance to cover specific contingencies. Assumption of a mortgage mortgage assumption is the process of one borrower taking over or assuming another borrower's existing home loan. When you're assuming a loan, the outstanding balance mortgage interest rate repayment period and other terms attached to that loan often don't don't change. And there's something mortgage might make sense for a home seller who is finding it difficult to attract potential home buyers or for a buyer who is being priced out of the housing market due to higher rates. Then we have a junior mortgage, the idea of a junior mortgage, a mortgage that is subordinate to a first or prior senior mortgage.

So the senior mortgage, the junior mortgage, often refers to a second mortgage mortgage, but it could also be a third or fourth mortgage. So now we've got to think about, OK, what's going to be the hierarchy of the loans? If we have a second mortgage in place, then if there was a default on the loans, then who has priority? In other words, if there was a default to sell the home. What if you sell the home and you don't get enough money to cover everything that was supported, all the loans that were supported by the home? Who gets paid first, second, third and so forth is going to be important to the lenders.

Now, obviously, if you have the primary principal mortgage starting out, you're going to be concerned if if someone else takes on, if they take on another loan and they put the home as collateral, then there's going to be a concern, well, who has first priority and second priority and so on in the event that the loans are not repaid. So in the case of a foreclosure, the senior. First mortgages will be paid down first home equity loans and the locks are often used as second mortgages, junior mortgages often carry higher interest rates and lower loan amounts and may be subject to additional restrictions and limitations. So if you're on a second mortgage, the second mortgage may result in higher rates, because that would just make sense given the fact that they're taking on more risk because they're not going to be paid off in the event that loans aren't being paid.

First rate, if the loans aren't being paid, if the house is repossessed and then sold, they're going to get as much money as they can on the sale. But if they don't get enough money on the sale to pay off the loans, who's going to get paid first? The primary mortgage and then the second. So it should still be covered in the event that the house goes up in value and so on. But if there's a decline in the market, then there's going to be who gets paid first, second, third, and so on. So homeowners may seek a junior mortgage to finance large purchases like home remodel, college tuition or a new vehicle purchase money, mortgage and mortgage issued by the borrower by the seller of a home as part of the purchase transaction. May also be called a seller or owner financing.

This is usually done in situations where the buyer cannot qualify for a mortgage through traditional lending. A purchase money mortgage can be used in situations where the buyer is assuming the seller's mortgage. And the difference between the balance on the assumed mortgage and the sales price of the property is made up of seller financing. Then we have the subordination clause to the subordination clause, a clause in an agreement which states that the current claim on any debts will take priority over other claims formed in other agreements made in future. So, again, this has to do with the hierarchy of who has the claim in the event that there's going to be a default on the payment to have the bigger security.

So subordination is the act of yielding priority, meaning, you know, subordinating one claim in essence to another. So if there's a problem, what do you know, the higher claim will get paid first and so on. When a home is foreclosed and liquidated for cash, the first mortgage lender gets first priority on the sale proceeds. Any money that remains is used to pay down a second mortgage. And then the third and so on. The further down the mortgage tier, a claim it is, the less likely it will recover its loan amount to adjust the priority of a loan. In the event of default, a lender may demand a subordination clause without which loans take a chronological precedence.

So they're going to take the chronological precedence unless there's, you know, something a clause that's going to basically change that a subordination clause effectively makes the current claim in the agreement senior to any other agreements that came along after the original agreement. These clauses are most commonly seen in mortgage contracts and bond issue agreements. Subordination clause continued subordination clauses are most commonly found in mortgage refinancing agreements. Think of a homeowner with a primary mortgage and a second mortgage if the homeowner refinance is his primary mortgage. This, in effect, means canceling the first mortgage and issuing a new one. So now you've got mortgage one, you've got mortgage two out there.

They want to refinance the mortgage one, which already had the primary sequence. But you're basically now, you know, reformatting it. So then the question is, will that reshuffle the sequence in terms of the primary and secondary, since you're forming it at a later point in time, you're basically ending one agreement and starting another with the refinancing. What does that do to the ordering of first and second in the event that there's a default on the payment when this happens, the second mortgage moves up the tier two, the primary status and the new mortgage becomes subordinate to the second mortgage due to this change in priority.

Most first, lenders require that the second lender provide a signed subordination agreement agreed, agreeing to remain in its original secondary position. So if you're the primary lender and you're saying, hey, I'd like to give you a refinancing situation, but if I do that, I'm canceling my first contract, I'm putting in a second contract. And because it's made after your second mortgage with your other lender, it's going to put my claim subordinate to them. So traditionally, then the general idea was to be saying, hey, look, secondary lender, you are the secondary lender. We would like to refinance over here without losing our status as the primary status in the event there is a default.

You're not losing anything. You're still the secondary. Therefore, you know, you have a subordination clause that could keep them, you know, in the primary position. So once again, due to this change in priority, most first, lenders require that the second lender provide a signed subordination. Agree. Agreeing to remain in its original second position. Normally this process is a standard procedure of a refinance, so it should be something that it's a fairly standardized process. However, if the borrower's financial situation has worsened or if the value of the property has significantly declined. The second mortgage creditor may be unwilling to execute the subordination clause.

So normally, under normal conditions, standard practice would be that the second would say, yeah, that's normal practice, let's go forward. But if there's been a decline or something and they feel like they're taking on more risk, then possibly they would say no and not and not do that, which would have a problem with the refinancing. So if the second lien holder provides the subordination clause, it allows the primary mortgages on the same property to have a higher claim. So your legal rights in a foreclosure, if you fall behind on your mortgage payments, your lender could try to take back your property through a foreclosure.

Obviously, the process of foreclosing and then trying to reclaim the loan that they took out, that's the point of the mortgage of the lean that took place before initiating a foreclosure proceeding. Your loan servicer must send you a notice that the loan is in default and gives you a chance to get caught up and avoid foreclosure. You also have the right to challenge a foreclosure if you think your lender made a mistake or has violated the law. Mortgage recast happens when a borrower pays a large sum toward the mortgage principal and the lender recalculates the loan based on the new balance.

So if they also pay a large amount and they recalculate the loan based on the fact that there's been that large payment, when the lender recalculates the loan, they will create a new amortization schedule. An amortization schedule is a table of loan payments showing the principal and interest that comprises each payment until the loan is paid in full. We will be creating amortization schedules shortly. The primary benefit to the borrower of recasting a mortgage is the opportunity to reduce monthly payments, negative amortization loans or option adjusted rate mortgages. Option arms often have a mortgage recast clause. Part of the loan contract. Voluntary conveyance.

Voluntary conveyance refers to an elective transfer of title from one individual to another without adequate consideration. Consideration refers to the compensation which is expected in return for property. Without it, the conveyor should be prepared to offer a legal explanation for the transfer. So in other words, if you have voluntary conveyance, usually if there's a sale on the market, there needs to be consideration, meaning payment for two parties have to have a consideration. There should be no benefit to both parties. So if there's not, in essence, benefit to both parties, you kind of need to be able to explain the circumstances as to why that would be the case, because that would be unusual.

Not like a normal harmfully market transaction generally. And then the short sale, finally, a house is sold for a price that is less than the amount still owed on the mortgage, on the mortgage. So now you get a sale that happens for less than the amount of the loan, which is generally a problem, because then, you know, you may not be able to pay off the loan, because the point is you sell it generally for more and pay off. So it is up to the mortgage lender to approve a short sale. The difference between the sale price and the mortgage amount may be forgiven by the lender, but not always. The financial consequences of a short sale are less severe for the seller than a foreclosure.

So that could be an option in lieu of a foreclosure. We might talk more about this kind of situation at a future point. But obviously, when you're talking about the lender side of things, they have the home as collateral. If the value of the loan becomes higher than the home value, possibly because they gave a loan out with little down payment and or the market price of the home went down, then you have a situation where sale can't happen. Even at a market price, they're selling at the market price, but that market price is not high enough in order to pay off the loan. And then you've got a situation.

Well, what would be best for the financial institution in that case? They may still be it may still be beneficial for them to have the short sale take place, a sale that doesn't even cover the loan amount, as opposed to going through the process of the foreclosure, which could could be more tedious to go through on the bank side in which could be more detrimental on the homeowner side. So it's important for the buyer to calculate their costs and be sure there is room for profit when the house is resold.

Does The Bank Own Part of My Home NO

Real estate investment. Does the bank own part of my home? No. Get ready because it's time to raise the stakes with real estate. When talking to people about real estate, it's common to hear people say something like, the bank owns a portion of the real estate property due to the loan. Due to the mortgage, which is not exactly true. It's a fairly large exaggeration. But we hear it commonly. It's useful to be able to understand what people mean when they say something like the bank owns a percentage of the property. Also useful to understand what actual ownership means and the difference between ownership and basically the loan and the mortgage. So its basic scenario looks something like this.

You got the home cost five hundred thousand down payment, one hundred thousand. That means we have a loan and the property securing the loan of the 400000, that means that the 400000 that you owe the bank divided by the property value, five hundred thousand is 80 percent. You can hear people say, well, the bank owns 80 percent of the home. Again, not exactly true. It means that you financed 80 percent of the home you owe the bank, then the amount of the four hundred thousand. And if you default on that, then the bank has some reBook and could possibly foreclose on the home. But that's substantially different than the bank actually owning the home, which will go into more detail in terms of what does ownership actually mean to kind of clarify this point. Before we do, however, let's just think real quickly.

Where might this have come from? I would think that this came from some kind of exaggeration that basically became a common kind of parlance, common talking points. At a later point in time, it would be something like if you lost a game of table tennis, a game of ping pong or something like that, and you lost badly and you said, man, I got killed. It's like, well, no, you didn't, you didn't actually get killed. You're exaggerating quite grossly there. You actually just lost the game of ping pong. You didn't actually die. We always exaggerate. Human beings always exaggerate. How often do we exaggerate? Like five million? Three hundred and fifty two percent of the time we exaggerate like all the time. So I think this would most likely have come from an exaggeration as well, where, for example, if you were to ask somebody, wow, man, this is a nice home.

And they were to say something like, yeah, but the bank owns 80 percent of it. That's an exaggeration. That means you financed 80 percent of it. The bank doesn't actually own 80 percent of it, but you could see how that would be kind of an exaggeration that's used so often that basically people see that and don't kind of see that it's an exaggeration any more often. So let's kind of think about that. Let's think about, well, what does it mean to actually own the home versus what does it mean to basically have a loan and the house as security? We talked about in prior chapters what a loan is, what a note is, what the mortgage is, what it basically means for the home to be secure. What does it mean basically to own real estate? What does that actually mean? And this we're going to be referencing down here that New York City bar legal reference service. You can look that up if you want to research on this further.

But ownership rights in real property, what does that mean when you own real property? You have certain rights that go along with the ownership, including. So we often hear this as kind of like a bundle of rights. What does it mean to own real property land and the things attached to it? In other words, it means that we have a bundle of rights with regards to that property. Now, when we look at these rights, as we go through these rights, we'll see that the bank doesn't have any of these rights to the property. What does the bank have the right to? They only have a right once we once we if we default on the loan, they have the right to the reBook, possibly due to the home being security. But that's much different than the bundle of. Right.

So let's look at these bundles of rights and just think of it in context of what the bank has and what we have. Right. The right to possession, obviously repossessed the home. Does the bank have the right to possess the home, even though we own all the financing worth 80 percent of the home? No, the bank can't possess the bank can't come into, you know, possess the home, come into the home and hang out on our property or something like that without our permission, because we own the home. They don't own the home. So the right to control again, the bank doesn't have the right to control the property.

If they actually owned 80 percent of the property and we wanted to say paint the house or something like that, the bank could come in and say, you know, I think you should paint it blue and we own 80 percent. So we have the controlling interest. You know, you should paint it blue and like no bank you don't own. We're not going to. I don't have to paint it blue because if you're going to redo the floor and carpet or hardwood, the bank would be like, you know, I prefer a carpet that. No, you don't. You don't ask the bank that because they don't own 80 percent of the property. They have no. Right, you know, to be able to do that. Right. To use and quiet enjoyment. So obviously, again, the bank doesn't have 80.

Percent interest, they can't use the property, so like you couldn't come home one day and the banks like, yeah, we got some new employees at the bank over here and they didn't need it. They needed a place to stay. So we just told them, since we own 80 percent of your property, that they could basically stay at your place for a while. It's not really your place because we own 80 percent of it. No, no. They can't stay at the place because you don't own 80 percent of the bank. You know, you only have limited access in the event that I was to to default on my payments of the loan. And even that reBook is restricted to foreclosure and selling the home in certain conditions in order to recap the loan. And you know that the right to allow others to use the used to lease it.

So, again, the bank can't be like, yeah, you know, I own 80 percent of it. We felt like we should lease out, you know, a couple of rooms over there. We thought that'd be a good idea. They know they can't you can't lease the home because you don't own the home bank and the bank doesn't own the home. Right. To privacy and to exclude others. If a bank can't be like, you know, we're not going to allow this person over to your home because, you know, no, the bank doesn't have the right to do that. Right to dispossession or transfer the property to someone else by selling, gifting or inheritance. So the bank doesn't have the right to say, I'm going to give, you know, 80 percent of the home to somebody else.

Now, they might sell the loan to somebody else. The loan might be transferable. But again, the loan isn't the same thing as the ownership interest. You know, that just means you'd be paying a different person under the same terms, in essence, of the loan generally. So the right to use the property as collateral. So, you know, the bank can't do, you know, do the collateral on the loan. You're using the home for basically the collateral. That's basically how the situation is set up, meaning the bank has reBook on the home. Only in the event, once again, that you default on the contract, you default on the payments, in essence, of the loan. So some more rights to continue your ownership rights to real property include the right to use the surface of the land called the surface rights.

So that's going to be the surface of the land. Again, the bank doesn't have the right to use any of that. You also have the right to use what is under the surface, such as oil, gas and minerals. So it's kind of important to understand what you want to understand and make sure that you have the rights or determine what type of rights that you have, the rights underneath the land, oil, gas, minerals, which, again, the bank doesn't have. 80 percent of this is called subsurface rights.

Your ownership rights include water rights or repairing rights, which are the rights to any water on the property and the right to make reasonable use of the flowing water that passes through or by your property. You have the right to use the space above the land, including the right not to have the air directly over your property blocked by buildings or adjacent properties. And when you acquire property, you must be careful to determine if any of these rights, such as the air rights, have been sold or pledged. So you've got to determine and make sure when you're purchasing the property, you know, that these rights are there.

But the idea here being, Of course, that property to own the property is these bundle of rights, which basically include the usage of the property, which, Of course, even though you own a loan to the bank and have a mortgage on, it doesn't mean that the bank has any of these bundle of rights. And therefore, to say that the bank owns some portion of the property due to the loan and the mortgage is really basically a gross exaggeration. But it's common. It's commonly used. So it's useful to kind of use it, but it's also kind of useful to know what the exaggeration is, what it means to have ownership, what it means to have a loan, what it means to have a mortgage.

Bankruptcy

Real estate investment, bankruptcy. Get ready, because it's time to raise the stakes with real estate. There are different chapters of bankruptcy we will be considering here. Chapter seven, Chapter 11 and Chapter 13. These will be definitional terms. We're going to be referencing Investopedia, which is a place you can go to further your research with regards to investment related terminology, starting with Chapter seven, Chapter seven being the classical type of bankruptcy, bankruptcy being something we think we're generally thinking of as a liquidation type of process. In other words, if you have a business or an individual in a situation where their income, their cash inflow is not sufficient to pay off their debts, then it becomes unsustainable.

They may then look into the option of saying, well, is it possible for me to liquidate, meaning move not just to the income accounts, but to the balance sheet accounts, the assets that we have, liquidate the assets and then pay off the creditors and hopefully then get a clean slate as much as possible after that point in time. Note that if you're on the creditor side of things and someone says, hey, look, I don't have the income in order to pay you, I can't pay you because I don't have the income sufficient to do so, you can imagine them saying, hey, look. Well, what do you have on the balance sheet side of things? Do you have any real property over there, over there? You know what kind of car you have? You have a hundred thousand dollar car or something like that.

Are there things that you could actually sell or liquidate where you could actually pay off the obligations? That's what, you know, the creditor would basically mean they would be thinking, well, you could actually pay off the obligation if you do have non-liquid assets that you could then liquidate. And generally, when you're thinking about the normal liquidation process in a bankruptcy, the concept would be to take whatever assets are there, liquidate them, and then pay off in accordance with the ordering of the creditors that you owe. And then hopefully in doing so after that process, then having more of a clean slate at that point in time. OK, so Chapter seven, bankruptcy is sometimes called liquidation bankruptcy. Business is going through.

This type of bankruptcy is usually past the stage of reorganization and must sell off assets to pay their creditors. So when you're thinking about bankruptcy, the first thing you generally want to think of would be, well, is there some way that I can reorganize? And some of the other bankruptcy procedures, you know, are more of a kind of a reorganization type of bankruptcy. The first thing that you might do as an individual and note here, the process works similarly for individuals. You might first go to the creditors and say, hey, instead of going to bankruptcy, is it possible to go to you and say, look, it's not sustainable for me to basically pay off these debts? Could we possibly work something out? And many times the institution has an incentive to work something out if they agree that it's also unsustainable to pay off the debt due to the fact that if you go through bankruptcy, simply the costs of going through bankruptcy are going to drain some of the assets as well.

And the creditors are not going to get as much due to that. So it's in their best interest oftentimes to work with you to try to reorganize so that you can pay off your debts. But if you can't do that, then you go through the bankruptcy, then decide, obviously, which type of bankruptcy you would want to be doing. Chapter seven is the classic liquidation bankruptcy, but does have problems due to the fact that you would have to liquidate things like possibly real estate through the bank, through the bankruptcy process. So the bankruptcy court appoints a trustee to ensure that the creditors are paid off in the correct order following the rules of absolute priority.

So then what they would do, obviously, is you'd say, OK, we're going to liquidate everything and then we're going to basically try to pay off who you owe in accordance with the priority. And whoever doesn't isn't up high enough on the list in order to be paid off before the assets are gone. It's going to be left out. They're not going to get paid. Right. So then the priority of the creditors now is they're going to be, you know, trying to be on the top of the list here. So secure debt takes precedence over unsecured debt in a bankruptcy and is generally first in line to be paid off.

So if the debt is secured, which, Of course, if you're talking about a mortgage on a home or something like that, the home being security, then that's the point that if you were to liquidate it, then you would think the bank would be, you know, fairly high on the list there to be repaid for its loans issued by banks or other financial institutions that are secured by specific assets, like a building or a piece of machinery or examples of secured debt, whatever assets and cash remain. After all, the secured creditors have been paid, are pooled together and distributed to creditors with unsecured debt. So anything that doesn't have the collateral whatnot is at the end of the line. They're more likely not to get paid because the cash is going to run out after a liquidation at some point.

That's why you went into bankruptcy. So continuing on to qualify, the debtor can be a corporation, a small business or an individual. Individuals are also eligible for another form of bankruptcy, Chapter 13. So Chapter 13 is the other kind of bankruptcy to individuals that's quite common, which we'll take a look at briefly in a second. Obviously, these are just a brief overview of the bankruptcy. Before we do so, let's take a look at Chapter 11. Bankruptcy may also be called reorganization or rehabilitation. Bankruptcy is the most complex form of bankruptcy and usually the most expensive. And that's why basically individuals usually don't use the Chapter 11, usually something like a Chapter seven or Chapter 13.

It is most often used by businesses rather than individuals, including corporations, partnerships, joint ventures and limited liability companies, or LXS. Chapter 11 gives a company the opportunity to reorganize its debt and try to reemerge as a healthy business. So instead of basically liquidating, which would be, you know, take out the business here. They're trying to reorganize with a Chapter 11 process. A case starts with a filing of a petition and a bankruptcy court, the petition may be a voluntary one filed by the debtor, but the petition can also be an involuntary one filed by the creditors who want their money. So the creditors may actually initiate here.

And then if you go into bankruptcy, then the process would be you got that trustee that's going to help. The third party is now involved in the process. So the debtor will remain in business while taking initiatives to stabilize its finances. And action may include cutting expenses, selling off assets and attempting to renegotiate its debt with creditors. This happened under the court's supervision. So now you have the supervision of the court, which is trying to be that third party that's trying to reconcile between the two people and get the finances back under control. So Chapter 13 bankruptcy. So now we're moving to Chapter 13 as part of the financial reorganization of Chapter 13.

A debtor must submit as well as follow through with a plan to repay creditors, outstanding creditors within three to five years. So three to five years. Chapter 13 bankruptcy may also be called wage earners plan, individuals paid and agreed on monthly amounts to an appointed trustee. So you got that third party trustee basically involved here to try to try to facilitate this process. Who should be impartial? Then the Chapter 13 versus Chapter seven, remember, these are the two that would generally be involved. If you're thinking about an individual situation, generally, Chapter 11 usually being for businesses more likely. Chapter seven is the most common form of bankruptcy because it allows individuals to erase their existing debt and start afresh.

So when you're thinking about classical bankruptcy, you would think about, OK, I'm just going to wipe out everything, I'm going to pay everything off, I'm going to liquidate everything. I'm going to pay everything off and start fresh. Problem with that is if you have substantial fixed assets, which could include real estate liquidation of those items are often something that people are reluctant to do to start over completely. And so that would be a limitation on Chapter seven, possibly. However, Chapter seven filers are often required to surrender their home, and that's generally a problem for many people. So once a Chapter 13 bankruptcy is initiated, any home foreclosure proceedings may be ceased.

Time Value of Money

Corporate finance chapter time value of money. Overview. Get ready. It's time to take your chance with corporate finance. Primary uses of time, value of money, a concept note that we can think about the time value of money concept as a type of tool. And then the question, Of course, is when would we want to use that tool? And what benefits would we get from using that tool? So typically, if we're talking about a cost benefit analysis for future benefits and current spending, that's one area where the time value of money is often useful. As human beings, we could be quite good, oftentimes just with intuition, really to make short term decisions. But when we're thinking about long term decisions, especially those where we have current spending that's going to be involved and long term gratifications, the benefit in the future, then we might then we're not as good at making those decisions.

Just intuitively, it's better to have a formal process. So, for example, if we're putting money in today for some type of capital expenditure, we're building a new plant. We're buying a piece of equipment that's going to be used. It's going to help us to generate revenue at a long point in time into the future. Question then, Of course, is, well, is it worthwhile to put the expenditure in today for the gratification that's going to happen in the future through added revenues in the future? In order to figure those types of things, we have to take into consideration the time value of money, helping us to put together a more formal type of decision making process. Capital allocation just in general could be useful with regards to the time value of money as well.

Again, anything that's going to be a little bit further into the future in terms of how we're going to be financing our organizations loans and whatnot, that could be taken into consideration. We want to make sure that we're taking into consideration the time value of money concepts with and not just from a managerial type of standpoint. You can kind of separate what you're thinking about in terms of a managerial standpoint. If you're talking about the Day-To-Day kind of management type of concepts, they're typically going to be concerned with spending you're at when you have that hat on right where you can turn. We're concerned with meeting our current obligations and doing what we need to do to meet those current obligations.

And then, Of course, when we're looking at those types of decisions where we have a longer term horizon, then that's when the time value of money becomes more and more applicable. That's when we often need to have more formalized tools to help us with those types of decisions, because there's a lot more factors involved. There's a lot more uncertainty that could be involved and the decisions that we are making. I have a longer term impact, so we need to be more careful on those types of decisions, in other words, with those types of decisions. We want to make sure that we kind of understand the concept of measuring twice and cutting once to get it right.

The first time would be better than if you're talking about other short term decisions where you have more leeway to basically learn through trial and error and make a lot of mistakes and then and then learn the best concepts as you go so we can break these time values of money into four different categories. And then we'll go into some more details about each of those categories. And then, Of course, the way to get these down is to just work practice problem after practice problem. We will have a lot of them in multiple different formats. So you can understand when to apply the time value of money, how to calculate the time value of money. Understanding that other people might do the same calculations in different ways.

They might make different assumptions within them. And you want to be able to recognize what is going on, no matter what assumptions are being made and what type of calculation they're using in order to make their analysis. So we could have a future value of a single amount. That's going to be a situation where there's the value of an amount that grows at a given interest rate over a set period of time. So if we're talking about a situation where we have some amount here and we're thinking that if we put it into a particular investment you can think about or if we put it into a particular thing, it's going to be growing at a fixed amount. So then we can then project into the future where we will be in the future amount. What's going to be the future amount if we take this lump sum and you can think of it most easily as an investment.

If we put the investment in there and it grows at a fixed rate and we just put one lump sum amount, not multiple amounts, which would be like an annuity, but just one lump sum, then where would we be at the end of some set time period? So if we have those fixed variables, we have the rate, we have the fixed time period that we're going to be putting into place, then we can figure out where we will be in terms of the future value. Then we have a present value of a single amount type of calculation. That's going to be something like a payment to be received in the future is worth less in today's time.

So that would be a situation, for example, if we're going to get paid in the future, for whatever reason, we're going to have a payment that happens not today, but at some point in the future, whatever the stated rate is for that payment, whatever the stated amount is, we need to basically bring it back to the current day, to the current. And so what we want to do is present value, then that single amount of the payment and you can imagine this kind of thing happening in a revenue planning type of thing as well. So if we make a certain investment, we're going to receive some revenue in the future that we would have to assume that would happen in the future and then present value that back into the current dollars once again, to make our decision making process to see if it would be a relevant thing to do.

Now, these are the single amounts, and we have to keep in mind the single amounts versus the annuity amounts. So we've got four concepts that will be in place. We've got the future value of a single amount, present value of a single amount. And then we have the same for annuities. So if we had so you can think about an annuity as basically a series of payments. So if we have a series of items that are going to be the same amount in the same period, like every year or every month, and we have the interest rate the same, those things fixed, then we might be able to simplify our calculation here by using an annuity type of calculation. So the future value of an annuity, for example, relates to a series of payments, compounds.

Each individual payment into the future then adds up the payments. So we could then think about the most common kind of scenario that pops up in most people's minds when they're thinking about the future value of an annuity, which would be like saving something for some goal in the future. So if I'm going to put a thousand dollars per year or per month or per some fixed time frame into a savings account, and I'm earning a standard rate of return on it, where will I be at the end of a set amount of time? So if everything is standardized in that format, then we can think about putting that in place with an easier calculation, which would be the future value of an annuity.

Then we have the present value of an annuity relates also to a series of payments, discounts, each payment back to the current period, then adds up the amounts. So now we're thinking about a series of payments. There's, you know, a thousand dollars going in each time. But we're trying to bring those future payments back to the current day. We're not trying to project out basically where we will be in the future. We're trying to present value, bringing all those series of payments back to the current day. Now, note again, you can do this kind of calculation more easily. Whenever you see a series of payments, you're going to go, OK, I'm bringing it back to the current day.

If I'm bringing it back to the current day, I'm going to use a present value of some kind present value of an annuity, or we'll use or we'll use the present value of single sums. If you're trying to think about where you will be in the future type of calculation, then you're typically thinking about the future value of one future value of annuity. And then if you're thinking if you see a series of payments that are standardized, the payments are happening, you know, in a standard format and the rates are going to be fixed or in that time period and whatnot, then you might be able to use an annuity calculation, for example, a present value of an annuity, rather than taking each item as a present value of one.

In other words, you could think of, for example, a series of payments that you're trying to bring back to the current period as the present value of an annuity. Or you could just take each one of them as the present value of one and bring them back to the current period. Individually, the present value of a new annuity will be much faster than a calculation if using a mathematical formula to do it. But note that once we put in the factor of excel into the equation, then Excel can kind of put these together or any spreadsheet, Google sheets and whatnot can put these together a little bit more easily. And actually having a series of present values of one might be useful.

So then it kind of converts when you would use one or the other to like if you're using a book problem, it's going to be quite clear that they're going to say if it's set up as an annuity, they probably want you to use an annuity and you want to make them happy. So you're going to use whatever formula they use in practice. Then there might be some situations where you would want to use an annuity or not an annuity, possibly not based simply on the ease of the math, because now you have a spreadsheet to do it, but rather in terms of how much information it would provide to you and or how easy it would be to present that information to others.

Your goal is to sort the information out in such a way that it provides the most information and is as presentable as possible. So those are your options. And then you can have them as you work through the problems, you actually have a between these options, you could have some different kinds of ways that you can come up with the same number and share the same information. We will work multiple different examples and show multiple different ways that you can calculate these. Also, just realize that if you're working on a book problem, the incentive is for you to understand these calculations and the relationships. They might emphasize the math to get you to know the math, or they might not as emphasize the math, they might show you the math, but then want you to use basically tables.

To do it, if they use tables, that's because they're trying to get you away from the financial calculator so that you can basically do it without a calculator, which they might think you're going to you know, it's not fair to do with a calculator and they don't want you to have a financial calculator or you could do it with Excel worksheets that have that have a basic function for it, which is really useful in practice. Probably what I would recommend most in practice or you can use a financial calculator which used to be really highly used, but I almost think Excel might be outweighing it at this point in time, given the fact that you can actually do a spreadsheet on your phone at this point in time. But a financial calculator would be another method that you could do these calculations.

The fact that there's multiple different methods confuses people. People think they're doing different things, even though it's the same thing with just a different method. So we'll go through those methods with many of our problems. Just each problem we'll look at, we'll look at with multiple different methods. So you kind of get the idea of what is going on when you can use one method and another and when you might want to use one of these functions, an annuity or present value of one and whatnot in different situations as well. Bottom line is to understand this stuff, work problems, work problems over and over again, even the same problem. Just do it again. Keep on working on the problems.

Present Value

In this chapter, we want to introduce the concept of present value. The first image we want to have in mind when considering the concept of present value is to have two time frames, two time periods in which we have the same dollar amount. So if we have the same dollar amount given to us either now or at some point in the future, which would we rather have? Typically, most people, if we're asked this question, would we rather have our dollar today or our hundred dollars today, or we would rather have it in the future, would say we would rather have it now. I'd want my hundred dollars. Now, if we were to ask why you'd rather have one hundred dollars now than in the future. You might give some reasons. Such as? Well, I want to use it now.

I have things that I want to buy. Now I have costs that I want to pay for with that one hundred dollars at this point in time. You might also get some answers, such as? Well, this is a little bit risky. I'm not. How do I know you're going to give me one hundred dollars at some future point in time? The bottom line is that the one hundred dollars today is worth more to us than the one hundred dollars that we make at some future point in time. We could then ask the question, well, how much would we have to give at some future point in time for these two amounts to be equal for us to value the one hundred dollars today equally to the amount that we would receive at some point in the future in order for these two amounts to be equal to us and value the future dollar amount, if we were to receive money in the future, would have to be higher than the current dollar amount. In other words, for us to make the decision to accept future money as opposed to today's money, we would expect that the future money is going to have to be higher.

It's going to have to have some higher dollar amount. So that's the first kind of image we want to think of when considering the present value of money. We typically think that the present value of the money is going to be worth more than the future value. So we have the same hundred dollars today, the same hundred dollars at a future time, that today's hundred dollars will be worth more. If we want even amounts to us, the future value will have to be a higher dollar amount in order to be worth the present value to us. There are a few reasons for that. One is just the fact that the value of the dollar will go down, so the value of the dollar will decrease over time.

That's due to inflation. Inflation is generally between one and five percent. So we can purchase less stuff with those dollars. That's one item that will decrease the value. The other is that there is usually some risk and or if we had the money today, we could invest that money someplace else and get an investment or a return on it. And therefore, the value would be greater today because we could use that money to either generate more money or get value from it by spending it. So if we had it today whether we spend it or not, it would be doing something for us, it would be working for us in some way. And that would be another factor that would increase the value today, as opposed to a future value for us to think about this numerically than we would have to think about some type of interest rate we would apply. This is going to be the formula that we'll think about with regards to present value.

So when we think about present value formulas, we're thinking about a future value out here. We have a future dollar amount that we want to bring back to present values. This is going to be important for capital projects, because typically we're going to talk about outflows or inflows that will happen in the future. We're going to get money in the future, let's say, and we need to bring it back to today's dollars so that we can measure it as of today's dollars. So we're going to get future outlays. We're going to have to measure them in today's dollars. So whatever the cash flow that we get five years from now, if we bring it back to today's dollars, it's going to be worth less as we compare to today's dollars and compare our investment to the cash flow.

So here is our formula P equals F over one plus I to the end. We're not going to spend a whole lot of time working on a lot of problems with the formula, because in practice and in schools, we often use other methods, such as annuity tables or excel to calculate these formulas. So if you're in a class, you may want to ask, are we going to need to know what the formula is and calculate with the formulas, or are we going to be using tables, will take a look at these different ways to calculate the present value for a few different reasons. One is that you want to be able to see them in these different formats, and know that they're not going to be different animals altogether. They're not different things.

They're all the same thing. They're just different formats to calculate it. When we go to the annuities, again, most schools don't require you to calculate the annuity with the formula, but give you other types of calculations so you can put your mind to other types of things, such as the concept of capital budgeting. And when we move to excel, we'll often use the formulas as well. And the present value, present value of annuity formulas will be very similar, as we will see. If we consider this time frame to be one year and we say that the future value we have is 220 future value, that's how much we're going to receive a year from now, and we plug this into our formula. P equals two hundred twenty over one plus point one. Ten percent is going to be our rate for one year.

We're going to get the two hundred and twenty. And if we want to prove that type of calculation, we could say, all right, let's reverse this. Let's say this is our present value. Multiply that times the 10 percent rate that's going to give us twenty dollars. The two hundred plus the twenty is going to give us the two hundred and twenty so we can kind of prove our calculation. If we wanted to see this for two years, let's say this is a two year time period then and we plug our numbers into our formula. We're now going to say that the future value is to forty two. To make this consistent. So the future value is forty two. We want to present value to forty two over one plus point one to the two for two years. That's going to give us two hundred dollars.

So if we see that in terms of our thought process, we can say, all right, if we have the two hundred starting with and we went through two hundred times, ten percent is twenty plus the two hundred is two hundred and twenty four year, one year to two hundred and twenty times the ten percent is twenty two twenty two plus two hundred and twenty is the two forty two. So you can kind of see how this is being worked together, how we can see this calculation formating. That's how we would take a look at it in terms of a formula. More common in schools is to use the charts. So when we think of a chart like this, there's typically four of them to present value charts to future value charts.

The reason they're very useful is because they don't require us to do the formula. Most of the financial accounting and managerial accounting is more concerned with our decision making process than the math involved in the formula. And when we go to annuities, the math, like we say, gets a little bit more complicated. It's easier to use the charts and it's going to be more the way we're going to be doing it in practice, typically. You can also use a calculator that's very simple and therefore don't need any complex calculator that could do other things on a test that possibly schools don't want. Therefore, we use charts instead of calculators and instead of excel in school, obviously in practice, Excel is probably the best way to go. And we'll take a look at that in an example shortly. So the chart, remember, there's four of them.

You want the present value charts. We're currently looking at the present value of one. So one number in the future, we're pulling back to the present value as opposed to a series, an annuity. So if you have a series of payments, that would be an annuity. The other way you can think about is, Of course, that these need to be, you could see they're all less than one.

So that would make sense because, Of course, if we're pulling a future value number into the present, it's going to have to be less than the future value. So we're going to multiply times something less than one. The rates will be atop the periods on the side. On the left side, we're looking at 10 percent and we're looking at two years.

So 10 and two years. Now, these periods could be in years. That could be in something other than years. Just note that the years need to coincide with the same rate. So in other words, we usually think of the rates in terms of years. If we were thinking about a monthly rate, we might have to take the rate divided by 12 so that we get the periods end. The year at the rate will line up together. So now we've got the point eight to six four. So that point eight two six four, if we take the 242 times point eight to six four, that's going to give us our two hundred. That's typically the format that we will use in many test questions.

Normally the question will be asking us for the present value, and we're considering the present value calculation. But it's possible for us to have this formula and be looking for something other than the present value. So normally we'll be solving for present value, but we could be solving for the interest rate. So if they give us, in other words, the present value and they give us the future value, and then we might solve for the missing factor in that case, which would be the interest rate, or it's possible that we might be solving for the number of periods so they could give us all the other data and we would need to solve for the number of periods to do that. We could use a formula to do that, if possible, to do that with tables, and we'll show a function to do that within Excel as well.

So Excel is the third way and the best way to really look at the same type of data. So we've looked at it in terms of a formula. We've looked at it in terms of tables. Now, Excel is usually the way that we'll see it in practice. And we really want to know within Excel, the present value and the future value formula. So we'll take our same data up top. We have the periods to the future value to forty two, so we're imagining we're going to get two hundred and forty two, two years in the future. What's the present value at a rate discount rate, the 10 percent. Given that data, we could go into Excel. We can go in. The formulas tab, we can go into the function library, the function library group, and then we can insert a function.

This insert function is where we can search for different functions. So if we type into this field, we want present value. We're looking for the PVB. And after a while, you should get used to just presenting Peevey. That's what we're going to use. You're going to see it in references all the time, because that's often the shorthand present value. So that's the formula we want. If we select that, then we're going to have a formula dialog box which will help us to process this formula. So the rate is the first item we need. It's going to be before Encel becomes four, so four is 10 percent. And then the number of periods is the next item we need. That's in Selby two, which is going to be the two dollars.

So it's and so be to the payments is zero. That's the tricky thing with this, because we're going to use the same Peavey formula for the present value and the present value of an annuity, and therefore we'll use the same fields. The payment means annuity payments, and there are none because we're not making systematic annuity payments. We'll take a look at annuity payments in the future. Therefore, that's zero. And this one. Notice how it's not bolded because it's not used in every function. This one is going to be what we use in the present value of one function, which is in Selby three B three is the amount of the 242. So that's what we're going to have. It actually gives us the answer. It's going to be two hundred so we can see the answer down below. And then once we enter this into the field, we'll get our answer.

And this is the way we would see it. If we wanted to just type it in as a function, which once you do it a few times, is pretty, pretty nice to do. It's a little bit quicker. I'm going to say equals. And we say negative because it'll flip the sign. If we don't put a negative, it'll come out as a negative number if we want to make it a positive number. We could put a negative before the brackets. And then notice this little dialog box down here that helps us to work through it. So when we're on before it's going to say that's the rate we're looking for, the rate. And so we're going to say, alright, before the rate. So that's up to 10 percent. And then when we say karma, that just means the next function, which is in PR. That's this item.

It says we need that. That's the number of periods. So it's two. So two is in P two. So that's in B two. Number of periods comma to the next function. And then we have the zero because we manually entered the zero, because, again, that's an annuity payment. This isn't an annuity. This is the present value of one comma. And then we have the future value, meaning this is the amount that we're going to get in the future that we need to present values. There's the 242 that's picked up in Selby, three of the 242. And so that's going to give us if we hit enter, that will give us our function, which will be the two hundred. Now, we also want to show this other information that will be the goal sought.

Remember, we said that it's possible that we have all the data except for the interest rate or all the data, except for the number of periods. And then if we have all the factors except one, we could just solve for that missing factor. We could do it with the formulas. In practice, it's nice to know the major formulas, which is going to be the present value of the future value. And then we could use a tool called goal seek instead of memorizing three formulas for every possible unknown. And these functions, we can use the one formula, present value, future value, and then use a goal if we need to solve for any other item. And that's one method that you can go through and that will simplify at least the amount of things that you have to memorize.

When you think about these types of problems. So how would that work? Well, if we have this data, let's say we had the periods, we had the amount, and then we don't know the rate. Let's say we know what the present value is, but we don't know what the rate is. So this is the one factor we don't have. We could plug that into the formula and then solve for the missing factor. Or we can tell we can basically tell Excel. I'm just going to guess the rate here. I'm going to put whatever the rate is here, and then I'm going to put our formula. This is going to be the PV formula here. And then we'll just tell Excel using goal seek. And I'm just going to explain it here. And you can go to the practice example problems where we'll actually do this in Excel. You can use Goldstar so you can say, hey, go seek Excel.

I would like you to change this cell to be what the answer is. Two hundred by adjusting the rate. And because there's a formula in here that takes into account the rate, it will then figure out what the difference should be. In other words, it'll test whatever the cell needs to be in order to make the cell what we told it to. Be 200 and it'll basically work that problem out. So that's one way we can basically solve any other factor, any missing variable using only one function, one equation within Excel. And we can do that here, too, like if we don't know the number of periods, but I know the amount. I know the rate and I know this is 200. Then I can say, well, let's use the present value formula.

I'm not just going to type two hundred in here and then look for a formula up top, because I don't know the formula for the number of periods. I don't want to know another formula. I just want to use the present form value formula to figure out the number of periods. Well, I know this is two hundred. I'm going to put in the formula for present value here, and then I'm going to use it . You can say, hey, excel, which you fill in, make this two hundred by changing this cell. Do whatever you have to do to that cell to make it two hundred.

And it'll obviously pick two years in the cell in order to make that two hundred. So that's going to be one useful tool. The reason we want to go over this and again, you could take a more detail on that in the example problem where we actually show this within Excel, is that by doing that, you can memorize basically one formula, the present value function. This function, this box presents value. The PV will be used for the present value, the present value of an annuity. And then you can also use that same formula to solve for the interest rate or the number of periods without having to learn multiple different different formulas and functions with the use of Gosuke. It's also very useful in many other areas.

Present Value Months as Period

In this chapter, we will take a look at the present value of a single summer using months as the period as opposed to years as the period, this is going to be our information. Up top, we have the number of periods which will be five. This time, however, in terms of months rather than years, as those five periods, we have the amount. Ten thousand. We have a rate of 12 percent. Few ways we can do these types of problems, ones with formulas and others with tables. Another is with Excel. We're going to take a look at Excel and the tables here. You'll note the table to the right. We see the rate up top. We see the periods to the left hand side. Neither of them show what type of period.

In other words, are we talking years? Are we talking this month? What are we talking about? Well, as long as we use the same item for both the rate and the period, we should be good. We want to use months. And therefore, the periods are what they are. They're going to be three months. We need to then change the rates to coincide with the months. That means we're going to take the 12 percent and divide it by 12 to get the monthly rate. And remember, whenever you see a rate typically, unless stated otherwise, it means a yearly rate. That's the default that we talk about. And that's going to give us usually our rates that kind of look reasonable. Types of rate that we talk about, a monthly rate we get very small rates, we start getting decimal rates and whatnot.

So therefore, we typically default to a yearly rate. If we want to know the monthly rate, then we have to take that divided by 12. Also note that we don't see this too often in book problems, because if they're forcing us to use the tables, then they don't want us to have something that's going to be uneven, because then if we can use tables. So therefore, in practice, this happens more often. Excel. We don't, it doesn't matter if we have an uneven percentage. That's OK. So I'll just note that in a book problem, that's why you don't see it as much, although it might be there in practice that we need to have periods that are going to be less than a year. So we'll take the twelve divided by twelve. That gives us one percent.

One percent being the percent three or we're at, what, five during the periods. And that's going to give us this point nine five one five and we'll have our ten thousand as the amount multiplying that times point nine five one five. And that gives us the present value nine five one five. Now we can also do this in Excel, Of course, Excel if we have our present value function, same present value function only difference now being we'll take the rate which is going to be in B for that 12 percent, and then we will divide that by 12 the number of months in a year. And that's going to give us the 0.01 or one percent then in the number a period that's going to be B2, which is five periods. So that will give us the five.

And then the payment amount is zero, because we're not talking about an annuity. We're going to talk about our present value in a single sum. So the payment is zero and then the future value will be three. So we're in B three. That's the future value, the 10000 that will give us our result here. It is being shown in a negative way. It's not even as well. That's OK. It's in a negative excel will then round it to whatever we decide to round it to. In this case, a whole number, nine five one five. Now, we can also type that out, Of course, with an excel in this format equals negative. And I put a negative in front of the P in order to flip the side, just to make it a positive result in numbers. And that will give us the rate.

So the rate is Defour and B four. And then we'll divide that by 12, the number of periods, comma. The next function number of periods is two. So then within the two five period comma, and then we'll have the payment, which is zero. There is no payment here. And then comma. And finally, we have in B three is going to be the future value. So we want to take the future value, the one sum, which is the future value, as opposed to payments, which we would use in the annuity.

Future Value

In this chapter, we will consider the concept of a future value. When considering the future value, we want to keep the same picture in mind we had with the present value. Obviously, these two terms are somewhat related to present value, future value, that picture being. If we had a hundred dollars today or a hundred dollars sometime in the future, which would we prefer? Typically the one hundred dollars today, the idea being that the money that we get today is worth more to us than the money in the future. And therefore, if we were to equate these in terms of value in the future, the dollar amount would have to be higher than the present dollar amount in order for these two values to be equivalent. That could be due to the value of the dollar going down due to inflation or to what we could do with the dollar purchase, get value at this point in time, or invest increasing the value of the money.

For practical purposes, we often think of the future value calculation in terms of investments. In other words, if we had a hundred dollars today, what would it be valued at in the future in terms of future value dollars if we were to get some type of return on it? In other words, if we had one hundred dollars today and we were to invest that one hundred dollars, how much would it be in the future? Note that when we're into the future and we count the amount of money we're in the future, dollar amount, we're at future dollar values. And therefore, it's often useful to think about the future value in terms of application, usually with regards to some type of investment.

We have money now. At what rate will it be to get some amount of money in the future? That amount of money in the future is in future dollars. Here's the formula for future value and will go through a few different scenarios in terms of how to calculate the future value. We have the formula, we have the tables, we have excel. We want to know about all of them, even if we prefer one of the methods, so that we know that if we see any of the other methods, we're not talking about a different thing. This is a different animal. It's just a different way to approach the same thing so that when we see that different approach, we then can apply it.

We can use our own approach. We can see how things are working, formula being F equals P times one plus I or interest rate to the N or the number of periods. For example, if we consider our time frame to be one year. So we have two hundred dollars here. What's it going to be in one year or what's the future value at a rate of 10 percent? F equals our future value equals the two hundred times one plus point one to the N or two hundred and twenty. We can also consider the calculation in this format. If we start off with two hundred dollars and we say eight times ten percent, two hundred times the ten percent, it's going to give us twenty dollars that two hundred plus the 20 will give us to that two hundred and twenty at the end of this time period at the future value.

Now if we think of this as a two year time period, then we would have the two hundred dollars. We are starting with times one plus point one to the two. And that will come out to future value. Two hundred and forty two. So if we started with two hundred dollars two years later, we've got the 242 there value. The two forty two is valued at future value. And again, what does that mean? It means it's actually if we were thinking about an investment, we would consider we actually have two hundred and forty two dollars two years from now. That's in future value terms. Those are in future value terms, not in present value terms. And again, the 10 percent that we're getting might be a good investment. We might say that's a good investment.

We earned 10 percent. It might be over and above what we think the rate of inflation is. The rate of inflation might be something less than 10 percent. So when we consider present value and future value in terms of equivalent dollars, remember that we're usually talking about the idea of inflation, which is usually in normal times in the US, one to five percent. If we're thinking about the investment purposes, often taking into consideration opportunity cost, what would be a good investment, then we're considering the rate of return on the investment. So these forty two that we're considering out here, if we're considering this 10 percent, then to be an investment type return is what we would actually have in future value terms if we want to compare it to what we had at the beginning.

We may need to present value in terms of purchasing power, which might be at a rate of, say, five percent or three percent in terms of purchasing power. So the types of Turmel terminology that we use with a future value and the interest rate could be a little bit confusing when we start to consider the types of investments or the types of ways we use the future value formula. Now, we could do our calculation just to double check this, that we started off and we left off last time two hundred times. Ten percent, twenty dollars. That's 220 for a year or two. If we start at two hundred and twenty times ten percent. That gives us twenty two dollars. Two hundred and twenty plus twenty two dollars is two to forty two. So that's another way we could think about how we are. Yet from the starting point to the future value, two years later, the 242.

The other way we can calculate this, other than a formula, is with the use of tables. The tables will often be used in test type questions at schools, because it allows us not to have to use the formulas and it allows us to not use complicated calculators that maybe institutions don't want during test time. And therefore the tables will work well and are close to practice in practice. Of course, we probably would use Excel, I think is the best format to use in practice. So remember, there's usually four tables. If you're considering future value, you can eliminate the two present value tables. You look at the two future values. Are we thinking about the future value of one or an annuity? And here we're thinking about the future value of one, because we don't have a series of payments. We have the interest rates on the top. We have the number of periods on the left. The periods could be years.

They could be months. Typically, we're thinking about years, but the periods don't necessarily have to be years. They do, however, coincide with the interest rate. So we usually see that. I mean, we usually see that interest rate or whatever rate we're using at the yearly rate. So if you're talking about a monthly rate, then you want to coincide with a number of periods that are months. You'll have to take that yearly rate and divide it by 12. So in our case, 10 percent, we have two years. That's one point to one, one point to one. So if we see our calculation, we have the two hundred starting at the one point two to one from our table that gives us an hour to forty two. That's the second way that we can calculate it, often used in testing situations.

In practice, we will typically use Excel. Once we know what the formula is, we can solve for any missing variable. So obviously we can use the formula to solve for the future value. If we know everything else within the formula or if we know the future value, we can use the same formula to solve for the interest rate or we can solve for the number of periods we can solve for whatever unknown is there, given the information that we have. We can use that and solve for that using algebra. We can work with the tables to do that. We'll show how to do that with Excel as well. And that's going to be the most practical thing to do in practice.

In other words, you really want to know the future value function. You want to know the present value function. And then you can solve for the different items that might be unknown, such as the interest rate or the number of payments with those functions using a feature called the goal seat function. So first, we'll go through the process in Excel. This is the third way that we've looked at. We looked at the formulas. We looked at tables. Now we'll look at Excel. The most practical format in real life in practice gives us a lot more options, a lot more flexibility to work with these types of equations. So we find this formula in the formulas tab. We've got the function library group, and then we're going to go to the insert function.

This is going to be the way that we can search for functions and it's going to give us a dialog box that we can enter into that's helpful often when we're getting used to it. We could search for the future value. It's going to be f v. You might want to start to remember a future value is going to be f v. You'll see it represented as V, because it's going to be common probably because of the use of Excel. So here's our function dialog boxes where we're going to enter the data. This will help us to go through the data. We'll start off with the right up top. So the rate up top is in before. So we have cell B for. And that's going to be the ten percent or point one. It'll give you basically what is in that cell over here.

And then we have the number of periods that's in the cell, too. So in cell B two, we have two. And so B2 gets us to zero. That's the tricky piece to zero. But this is nice because note that the future value formula, the f the formula function will be the same for the annuity. It will be the same for the single payment of one. And that means we only need to know one function once we understand the difference between those two. And if we can combine that with the goal seq feature, we can also solve four different factors within the equation with just this one function as well. So if we can understand the fVI function and the difference between the usage of the payments versus the present value, we're doing quite well.

So we have the payment going to be zero. We would only use that if it was an annuity, if it had a series of payments, rather than just one payment at one present value payment. And then we have the present value. Notice, it's not Boldon, because it's not necessarily it's not going to be used in every kind of calculation. It would not be used if we had an annuity calculation. It will be used in this case because we're using the present value of one. That being the difference between these two. That's going to give us our answer of the 242. So here's our two forty two that it would result in through this function. Now, we can also see this function in terms of if we wanted to type it in. This is the actual. Formula that will show it's going to be equals.

I usually put a negative before the Evvy or else it'll give a negative number as a response, the negative before it will flip the side to a positive F the brackets. Then we're just going to follow our little dialog box down here. So it says rate rate is going to be here. That's picked up and before. So before is the rate comma just means that it's going to go to the next function, which is the NPR PR, which is the number of periods it's in B two. So that's going to be B two, which is two periods. And then comma. And that's going to give us our next function, which is the payments, which is zero, because it's not an annuity. So we just put in zero manually then comma. And the next item is going to be PJV or present value B three. So be three or two hundred.

And that's what it would look like in terms of just the formula view of this. Now, also note that we can't figure out if we have this formula, this function, this form F equals P times one, plus either the end we could solve for F if we know everything else. But if we have everything but the interest rate, then Of course, we can solve algebraically for the interest rate. Or if we have everything, plus the number of periods we could solve for the number of periods. We could do this algebraically, but we can also do it with Excel. And the way we do it with Excel is we can use this goal, seek features. So the goal is going to be over here in the what if analysis. And then you would go to goal seek and it's under the data.

So data, what if analysis, goal seek. And if you want a more detailed example of this, we'll have demonstrations within Excel. But the idea then being that we can only know or we only have to know, then the future value function. And we then can solve for anything, anything. That's unknown here. So if the only unknown is this item or the number of payments, we can use the same function and not learn three different functions, use the same one we can use, go seek to figure out the unknown variables so we won't go into the detail within the PowerPoint.

So if you want more detail, some examples of that, we'll have example problems that will actually be in Excel. Just note, what we want to do here, Of course, is to basically memorize the minimum amount that we need to get what we need to get done, done. That means we need to know the present value formula. And we need to know the future value formula. And that'll take care of the present value of one present value of an annuity, future value of one, future value of an annuity. And the unknown, if we know everything else with the use of Gorske, including the interest rate and the number of payments.

Future Value Months As Period

In this chapter, we will take a look at the future value with the use of months rather than years as the period. This is going to be our information up top. We have period five, this time in terms of months rather than in terms of years, the amount ten thousand. The rate is 12 percent. Three ways we can do this. We can do this with formulas. We can do this with the tables. We can do this with Excel. We're going to be taking a look at the tables and excel in this example. If we look at the table to the right, we have the rate and we have the period right up top the periods to the left. The main point here is that we don't see the rate per period.

In other words, what are we talking about, months, years or what not? What's going to be the period that we are using, not given in the table? We can use the tables as long as we use the same period in terms of the rates and the number of periods, the periods, we can't change on the table. It is what it is. It's going to be five periods, the rate we can change. So the rate we change by saying, hey, this is 12 percent, we want a monthly rate, therefore we can take that and divide it by 12. And that will give us our monthly rate. Note that in order to use the tables, because they only have even percentages, we can only do this if we had some monthly rate that was even to use the tables. And that's not always the case.

Therefore, the tables aren't always the best thing to use. And that's also why they might not have monthly types of periods within book questions if they're required to use the table and practice. We may well have months. It's not a problem for us to use fractions within an Excel type of calculation. OK, so we're going to take the 12 percent and divide it by 12. We'll get one percent per month. So here's our one percent per month. And here are the five periods. So we're going to have the amount of one point two oh five one zero.

So the amount is ten thousand, then our table amounts one point oh five one zero. And that's going to give us our future value. Ten thousand five hundred and ten. So again, that's going to be with the use of the one percent as opposed to the 12 percent, given the fact we're talking about months rather than years. That's the key point. If we look at Excel, then the same data is now in Excel. Future value, function f, the function that we will be using. Here's the function box right up top. The B four is going to be the cell. So here's B for that's going to be 12 percent. So there's R R, B four divided by 12. That's the key point. Now, if it was something other than an even number, then that would be OK for Excel. In this case, it's one percent.

So one percent is going to be what we have. Then we can have the number of periods is B to five of those to coincide with a five month monthly rate. And then we have the payment is going to be zero, this not being an annuity, but a single sum, present value, then B three, B, three being the ten thousand. The result is negative, ten thousand five ten. And then, Of course, if we show that in Excel, it's going to be recorded. If we want to flip the sign, we can put a negative in front of the future value. That's how I would do it. And that'll give you a positive number. In essence, taking in the balance, multiplying at times negative one. And then here we have the future value brackets. The rate, if we want to type it in this way, which we can, Of course, type it in this way as well, the rate being and be four.

So within before we have the 12 percent taking that dividing it by 12, the next function, we use a comma and go to the next argument, which is the number of periods. So that's going to be in B2. So B2 is B2 is five. And then we say, Karmah, go to the next argument, the number of the payment, that's going to be zero because this is not an annuity. We're talking about a single sum. And then the next argument and B three is going to be the present value. That's in B three. That's ten thousand.

Future Value vs Present Value

In this chapter, we will take a look at present value and future value and the relationship between them. To do that, we're going to take a look at these two sets of data and compare and contrast that calculation of the present value and future value. Now, remember that there are three ways that we can go about this. Typically, one with the use of formulas to with the use of tables. Three, with the use of Excel or some type of financial calculator. We're going to go through the concepts here. So if we have the amount of ten thousand dollars, the number of payments, five years, we're going to say in years in this case, and the rate 15 percent, this is what we need to calculate the present value.

If we were to calculate the present value, no matter what method we use, whether it be the formulas, the tables or excel, we would then get the present value of four thousand nine seventy two. Now, if we take that same present value and then use it as the amount that we're going to use the present value to calculate the future value using our same data or similar data, we're going to have the amount four thousand nine seventy two, the number of payments five years, and the rate 15 percent. We can then calculate the future value. And you could do this in Excel. We'll do this in Excel in our practice files as well. And that hopefully will just kind of solidify this relationship between the present value and the future value.

They're going to be, Of course, related formulas that we would get to the 10000, which was our original 10000 that we started with. Another way you might want to consider going through this data, just to solidify the relationship between present value and future value is going through the calculation starting at the place of year zero, which is going to be the four thousand nine seventy to the present value, and then get to year five through our calculation year by year. So if we take the rate then of one hundred and fifteen, this is kind of shortcutting it because Of course we're taking the 15 percent and then and then we're taking point one, five plus one, one hundred and fifteen percent, 100 percent plus 15 percent.

So you could calculate it such as four, nine, seven, two times point one, five. And then you would get four 748. And then add to that the four nine seven two and you get the five seven one seven or. And this is rounded five seven one eight. Or you can just take the one nine seven two times the 100 percent plus the 15 percent or the one point one five, one hundred and fifty percent to get that same one seven one seven point eight. And it's rounded to one seven 18 here. If we take that number times, another one hundred and fifteen percent. So five, seven, one eighth times one point one five. Then we're going to get in year two, six thousand five seventy five. So if we take that six thousand five seventy five, six, five, seven, five times one point one, five, four, year three, we get these seven, five, six, one.

So if we take that seven, five, six, one time, one point one five, we're going to get the eight, six, nine, six. And if we take this, Of course, we're rounding here eight, six, nine, six times, one point one five. We're going to get ten thousand. Of course, it's rounded. And so that kind of calculation can give you a better idea or an idea of this relationship between the present value and the future value of a better understanding, a feel for the formulas so that when you use them, you have a better idea of what's going to happen. What you want to do is have a good enough idea of what's going to happen, the relationship between them, so that if something or something goes wrong, you can say that doesn't make sense, obviously.

I'm going to go back through there and figure out what is wrong instead of blindly relying on the formulas, because we don't understand exactly how they work or what the relationships are. Once we have that information, we can go through the goal, seek and solve for other factors which might add to our understanding of the relationship between the present value and future value will do this in Excel examples. But note that if we have our information, everything except the interest rate we can use, go seek to find that. For example, if we knew the ten thousand the five years and we knew that the present value should be four thousand nine, seventy two.

Well, then we want to solve for the interest rate. We could do that with a formula and plug in everything except the unknown, the rate solved for it. Or we can use goal seek within Excel, which will in essence do the same thing we can tell Excel. I'm going to put in the present value formula here. The present value formula. And then I'm going to tell Excel.

Hey, Excel, would you make that present value formula that sells what I know the answer is for what it should be for nine seventy two. That's a known factor in this problem. What I don't know is the rate. So I want you to make it. Use that present value formula to make this number four thousand nine seventy two. By adjusting this rate, this rate is used in the present value formula.

And in doing so, it'll figure out, Of course, what the rate is, which will be 15 percent. And if we did that same kind of analysis down here with the future value, if I knew the amount either present value, if I knew the number of payments, and then the future value, we know as 10000, we can say, hey, I'm going to put in the future value formula here, let's put in the future value formula and then tell Excel, hey, the future I want you to make this future value formula are equal with 10000 by changing the rate. I want you to change the rate until this is going to be 10000.

And again, if we do that, it'll fix the rate or change the rate to 15 percent using a similar method. So if we go through some of these exercises, you can give us a better idea of a feel for these things. The relationship between present and future value recommends going through the Excel files and actually doing these exercises, and they'll give you a good feel for them, as well as learn the tool of things like goals, stick and the formulas.

Present Value Annuity

In this chapter, we will discuss the present value of annuities when discussing present value in general. We said we want to picture and we still want to picture when considering the present value of an annuity. The idea of having two time frames now and in the future, and the choice as to whether we would rather have the money now. Hundred dollars today versus one hundred dollars in the future. And we know that we would typically rather have the hundred dollars today. In other words, today's value is typically worth more if we have the money now. It would be worth more the same dollar amount in the future or thought differently. If we want to have the same value to us today and in the future, the dollar amount we have today will be less than the future dollar amount.

In other words, we would need to be given more money in the future to be equivalent to the less money that we would get in today's dollars. That's going to be the kind of concept, the central concept with present value and future value that we want to have in our mind. Now we want to differentiate the present value of a single sum. If we were going to present value just one number, taking a future value and bringing it back to the present value terms versus the present value of an annuity, an annuity means we're going to have a series of payments, we're going to have a series of payments, and that's going to constitute an annuity. Now, if we're considering an annuity like these hundred dollars, they would have to be an even series of payments.

So if we have an even series of payments over an even interval like yearly type of payments, then we can use an annuity formula, which is in essence just a variation on the present value type of formula. So we could do one of two things. If we had an annuity in this fashion in order to present value at one, we can use the old method we have and use and basically present value each year. ALSIP This represented three years of 100 dollars. We can present the value of each one of these years and then add them together using our present value formulas. Or we can use another technique, which would be an annuity calculation, and use an annuity formula in order to get to our calculation.

So in other words, if we took our present value formula, we can basically add together these three payments and say we have the present value of period one, period two and period three and add those together. So in essence, we're saying if we're going to get one hundred dollars a year from now, two years from now, three years from now, we're just going to apply the present value to each of those years, bring in all of those years back to the current dollar amount, the present value. And that's going to be one format that we can use to calculate this. And this is going to be useful with capital budgeting capital projects, because we're going to have cash flows out into the future and we're going to want to pull them back into the same basic dollar amount, the same time frame, today's dollars, the time at which we're going to make the decision.

So in this example, if the rate was 10 percent and we had the one hundred dollars, then we can add this into our Formula

One hundred over one plus point one to the one one hundred over one plus point one to the two to one hundred over one plus point one, two to three. And we get to the present value of 248. Sixty nine. So that's going to be kind of around what we should expect, because note that if we have the cash flow of one hundred times three, you would expect it to be three hundred if there were no time value of money involved. If these are the three payments and we want to bring them back to the current time period and we want to measure them in today's dollars, then you would expect it to be something under the three hundred dollar amount.

It's common to get a little bit confused about the present value versus the future value. So note, when we are thinking about the present value, it's useful to have a scenario, a common setting that we would put this context in. In other words, if we were thinking about the future value, we might be thinking, oh, these are going to be investments. We put in a hundred dollars each time period. We're trying to think about what the future value would be at the end of that time here. That's not what we're doing here. It might be best to think of an investment type of project where we're putting money in a hundred dollars in year one, a hundred dollars in year two and one hundred dollars in year three. And what we want to do is decide whether or not we want to do that in the current time period.

So we're trying to make those payments, although they don't all happen in today's dollars, in today's dollars, so that we can make the decision as to whether it's going to be a good idea or not. So when we think about the present value, it's often useful, as we will be doing with capital projects, to think of these outlays possibly as expenditures. We're making a payment in the future, payment in the future, payment in the future. We're going to pull them back to the current day and think about it in that fashion. Or you can think about this as income in the future, income in the future, income in the future, that we want to pull back to the current date and compare to an original in.

Estimate that we're going to be investing at this point in time, as opposed to a future value scenario, where we would think about us investing in something like stocks and bonds or something like that, typically where we would say we put a hundred dollars in, it's going to earn 100 dollars and it's going to earn and grow hundred dollars, and it's going to earn and grow and then get to the future value amount, the amount that we expect to have in future dollars at that time period, at the end of the time period. So our present value of an annuity formula is going to look like this. It's going to be a bit more complex here, Of course. And for this reason, in practice, we don't typically use the present value of an annuity for. We're going to use Excel or we're going to use a financial calculator.

Even in schools, they don't typically require you to fill out the formula or use the formula too much, because in practice, it's a lot more useful to know the concept and then use the tools, which usually includes Excel. So this is going to be the formula that you may have to use. And it's good to have an idea of it and know of it so that when you do see the formula in terms of chapters such as this, we can understand what it is and what it is in relation to the same types of calculations that can be done in other ways, including the tables which are often used in schools, because that allows us to use a simple calculator without having other kind of functions that they may not want in tests and still do it in a similar fashion as we might do in practice.

And then, Of course, in practice, we would probably use Excel would be the way that we would use this most often. And that's the way that you probably want to get most familiar with for practice. But again, you want to be able to see all of these different formats and be able to know these aren't different animals. These aren't different things. These are all the same things. And you can prove that to yourself by solving them in different formats. And then when you see them in different ways, they're not something that's going to be intimidating. You're just saying, oh, they did that with a fancy formula. I know what it means. I know how to do that. I can do it with a table. I can do it with Excel and get to the same numbers, the same concepts.

So here's going to be the table, which we often use. So there's three ways to do it. We've looked at a formula and then typically in schools, we're going to use these tables because that allows us to do how we would typically in practice and not have to use the formula. We're not concentrating on math in terms of math, for math sake. We're looking at applications and the tables help us to do that. So remember, there's four tables. Usually we're looking at present value tables. This one, we want the present value of an annuity. So anytime we have multiple payments that are the same, we may be able to apply the present value of an annuity. We've got the rates up top. We've got the periods on the left hand side. So we're going to be picking then the 10 percent and the three time periods.

So that's point four, eight, six, nine. And note, what we have here is something that we would kind of expect to have, right? Because we're talking about three periods. Three periods if we had one hundred dollars was our amount times three. That would be what you would think would be three times. And you'd have three hundred dollars because we're putting a hundred dollars in every year for three years. So in this case, it's got to be something that's lower than three, but above one, clearly, because we're talking about something that's going to have to be less than three hundred dollars to present value, discounting it at 10 percent.

We'll also talk more about this 10 percent and where do we get to this 10 percent in future chapters? That's going to be our discount at this point in time. So it'll be given now. We'll discuss where that comes from a bit more in-depth in a later chapter. So if we want to take a look at that, then we're saying the one hundred dollars times eighty two point four, eight six nine that we got from the table and that'll give us our two forty eight sixty nine same idea that we would get with a formula. And this is the way we would most likely see it, probably in schools and testing type of situations. Now, the most useful way to do it in practice will typically be excel.

And we really want to know the present value of an annuity, the present value of one. They're really the same functions.

They just are used a little bit differently, which is nice for us to be able just to learn that one item. So we're going to go into formulas. We're going to insert. We're going to go into the function library group, and then we're going to insert a function. This will help us to search the function if we don't know it or if we want to use the formula box to help us to enter it more easily, we can type in the present value. We're looking for the PJV, which has the same present value as a present value for one formula. We use the same function for the present value of an annuity, which is nice.

So once we know the difference in how to calculate them both, we can use the same PV function and that could save us some memory space on that. So we're going to say the rate is going to be the first thing we need. The rate was Encel before. So we have a B rate of 10 percent. So 10 percent given here. And then we have the number of periods that's. Sell to the number of periods we're saying years in this case, which will be three, so be two, we have three years and then we have the payment amount. Now, last time we didn't use the payment amount because we weren't doing an annuity. We were present. We'd won. We put a zero here.

And then we use the future value. If we were presenting value in one item, that's what we did. We put a zero and then we go down here. But the payments are there for an annuity. This is an annuity. We're going to be making payments. The payments mean that I will be making a payment each of these three years. In this case, three years, 100 dollars. We're going to make it three. One hundred dollar payments. Three hundred dollars in total. So we've got one hundred in B three. It'll give us the answer. It's going to be in the negative. And let's put a negative somewhere to forty eight point six eight. So there's our answer to forty eight six eight round into two forty eight six nine.

And then if we see this in basically our format in terms of just a function, if we could just type it into Excel, we'd say equals I usually put a negative in front of the PV to flip the sign. So that'll flip it from a negative result to a positive present value. And then we'll go through a little dialog box. We've got the rate first that's in before. So in P four, we have the rate 10 percent. Then we have the number of periods. So the number of periods is going to be B two. So then we have B two. And that, Of course, is three. And then we have the payments and the payments are going to be B three. So we have B three. And that, Of course, is one hundred dollars. And so that's the same thing as we did in the prior chapter. Now, in terms of a function, it's a little bit easier to enter this way. This is what will be in the cell if we were to use this dialog box as well.

Remember that we can use the same present value function now. We can use the same function for the present value, the present value of an annuity. And then if we need to look for some other factor within that formula, we can use the goal seek feature. So, for example, if we had this data up top, if we knew the number of periods, if we knew the payments, but we didn't know the rate and we knew what the present value should be, then we could basically say to excel. I want to use the present value formula here, use the present value formula to find what the rate would be. So we'll basically enter the formula here, and then we'll use goals that you can say, hey, tell us what the rate is based on the present value formula here, and we'll say, hey, excel, tell me make this number be what it should be by changing this cell.

And again, we could do the same thing down here for the periods. If that was the unknown, we could use Google stick to find this will do this in our Excel example problems. If you'd like to work through this using Google Gorske, we'll say, hey, here's the present value. We know that 10 percent, we know the payments are one hundred. We're going to enter the formula for the present value here and then ask Excel, Excel. Would you please make this be what it should be? Because we know the answer, but we want to use it in a formula by changing the periods, and then it'll change the periods in order to find the correct answer, which will be three in this case.

The point here is just to say that we can use the same present value formula then to have the same dialog box for a present value, present value of an annuity. And then we do not have to memorize other functions if we know everything except the period and we know everything except the rate, because we can use the same present value function and to find that. That's one way that we can find those items, all with the same use of the same function with it excel, which is nice.

Present Value Annuity Months as Period

In this chapter, we will take a look at the present value of an annuity with the use of months as the periods as opposed to years as the periods within our calculation here, here's going to be our data up top when you have the periods three, but this time months as opposed to years, we have the payments are going to be the ten thousand and the rate 12 percent. We could do this three ways. We could do it with a table, with formulas or with Excel. We're going to show the tables and excel if we look at the table to the right. We know that we have the rates up top with the periods on the left hand side.

Neither of them refer to any type of period, such as year or month, just telling us what the period is and the rate is what we need to do. As long as we're using the same period for the rate and the number of periods, then we should be OK. So the rate up top, then we want to make sure that we have the monthly rate. Typically, that's the thing that we will change. So the periods are going to be three in terms of months, we're going to say. And therefore, the rate we need to use needs to be in the terms of months. The problem is that the rate that we have here is going to be in terms of years normally. So we need to take that rate and divide it by 12.

Book problems often don't do this. They often have a yearly rate, because if we use the tables, it's going to be confusing because it could come up to something other than an even percentage. So to use an even percentage will use twelve divided by 12 to give us one percent. And obviously, we don't have this problem in Excel. And in practice, it's much more likely things don't work out perfectly. And we have a few months that we're going to have to calculate into our calculation as well. So we're going to have the percent. Then we have the number of periods three, one percent per month. And that's going to give us two points nine four one zero. So ten thousand two point nine four one zero.

Multiplying that out gives us twenty nine thousand four hundred and ten. Then we could see this in terms of Excel. Same data on the top left. We're going to put that into our worksheet, our function argument, bottom right. The rate then is going to be in a B four. So we have B four. That's going to be 12. And then we'll divide that by 12. And that's going to be what we'll do here. And again, it doesn't matter in Excel if it's not even so, because Excel will deal with the rounding. And we don't have the same problem as we do with the table. But this time it comes out, Of course, to the one percent. And then we'll take a look at the number of periods, that being three in terms of months, although it doesn't say it here, it will be in terms of months because it lines up to the monthly interest rate.

And then we'll have the payment, which is going to be in B three, and that will be the ten thousand. So then if we calculate that out, it comes out to the twenty nine for 09 once again. And if we see that in terms of the formula, it's going to be equal. I put a negative in order to flip the side rather than getting a negative result. We'll put a negative in front of the TV brackets. Then the argument will follow down here first, the rate before. So then before twelve divided by the number of months, 12 to get the rate per month. And then we've got the comma in the next argument, which is going to be the number of periods and B two, that's going to be three and B2 and then the comma. And then the payment, which is going to be in B three, that being the 10000.

Future Value Annuity

In this chapter, we will take a look at the future value of annuities as we consider the future value of annuities. We want to keep that same picture in mind that we had for the present value and the future value, that being our two time periods, either now or in the future. And the question of what we'd rather have the 100 dollars today or the one hundred dollars in the future, the answer obviously typically being we would rather have the one hundred dollars today, or if we want to think about this in a different method. The question being, if we want the same purchasing power as the money today or in the future, then the amount of money someone would have to give us in the future would have to be higher than the amount of money we would have today in order for us to value them the same.

That's kind of the core concept that we want to consider with the future value and the present value in the relationship between the two. When we're considering the annuity payments, then we're talking about a series of payments. So we have a series of items, a series of cash flows, those cash flows and set consecutive intervals such as here. So we have the same dollar amount and they're going to be in some intervals that are the same. Then we may be able to apply an annuity type of calculation. In this case, we're taking a look at the future value type of calculation. And if we put that into the scenario for considering a future value, the most common type of calculation or thought process or application of the future value is for us to think of this as some type of investment.

So in other words, if we were to put a hundred dollars in a year from now, two years from now, three years from now, then how much would we have at the end of that time period? And we could think about it as actually how much we would have three years from now in actual dollars at that time period, because that future amount is going to be in future dollars. So we're going to have those future dollars in that future time period, a now amount, as opposed to us taking these payments and bringing them back to valuing them at the current time period. So that's typically the scenario that we would want in our head. We're going to have a series of payments.

We're going to apply some type of interest rate. Remember that that interest rate might be considered the interest rate that we would have in order to account for the time value of money, such as inflation, the purchasing power going down. That would typically be in normal years between like one and five percent or in the case of an investment. We're considering how much value we can get within the investment. We might consider an opportunity cost, where we can put our money somewhere other than the investment to consider how much our investment would grow as compared to another place that we could put our money.

So that could be a little bit confusing when we think about the future value and the consideration of what it means to be a future value versus the present value, because obviously, when we consider the purchase, that future value and the rate that we're using, we're using the rate of return. Oftentimes when we're considering the investment, we invest in something, receiving a rate of return, the future value then will be the actual dollar amount at that future time period, that future time point. We can think of the future value of an annuity in terms of a formula. That formula can be derived from the future value formula of a single sum. In other words, if we were to think about this scenario where we had three cash flow payments, we had a hundred dollars in a year, one hundred dollars in a year to one hundred dollars in year three.

And we want to find the future value at, say, 10 percent being the rate. We could then take the future value for each of those time periods, add them together, and we would get a future value of 331, or we can use this formula up top, which will basically be derived from this concept and apply that information into our future value of an annuity. We can use this formula, which will be more simplified to one calculation rather than three. Or you can imagine this going out for a long extended period of time, in which case the future value formula would be useful to use. However, it is more of a complex type of formula. We don't often use it in this format in practice, because we'll use something like Excel or if you're in school, they'll usually use tables to do that.

They're often not going to make you use the future value of an annuity formula because it is a bit more of a complex formula. Our goal really isn't the math to understand the math behind it, but the application of it. So oftentimes within schools will be using tables. So the tables are useful because they allow us not to have to focus on just math, do in the formula, but on practical practice, although they don't make us use calculators that might have other functions that they don't want in tests, we can use a simple calculator and then use the tables, which are similar to what we would use. Practice, which would typically be something like Excel.

So remember, there's going to be four tables that you're going to basically be using and seeing. If you see this in a school problem and a test problem, you can look for the future value tables now so you can eliminate the present value tables and then you want to pick up the future value of an annuity. If you're looking for consecutive payments, payments, multiple payments that you're going to calculate with one calculation, we have the rates up top. We have the periods on the left hand side. We're picking up the 10 percent at the rate. Three years in terms of the numbers of periods, that is three point three. One is going to be the amount and note. That's kind of what we would expect it to be, because we have three payments. If we have three payments of 100 dollars times three, you would expect that to be three.

That's three hundred if there was no time value of money, no future value. And we're expecting it to be higher than that because we're value in it at a later date, at the later date. And you can think of it as an investment. If it's the later date, it's going to have to have earned some kind of return on investment. So it's got to be something a little bit higher than the three hundred. It's got to be something that's going to be multiplied by something higher than the number of periods,

periods or three. It's going to be multiplied by something a little bit higher than the periods you would think, given the fact that it's going to be the future value of money. If we do this calculation, then we're going to take our hundred dollars.

We're going to multiply it times a three point three one that we got from the table. And that gives us three thirty one. So the future value of these three cash flows then three thirty one. Now we've seen that happen two different ways. We use the formula, which we probably don't actually use in practice or even in test questions too often. We'll use the tables and test questions typically, and excel being the third option that we'll usually use in practice. You really want to know these formulas within Excel, within Pract. We're going to be in the formula Tavs or in the function library group, and we're selecting the insert function. This is where we can search for the appropriate function that we want.

If we search the function, we're looking for the same function. The future value, the future value is used for both the future value of one and the future value of an annuity. We're just going to use different functions within that system. So we want to be able to know that it's nice that that's the case, because we can only use one future value, and then we just need to know how to apply them to the future value of one versus the future value of an annuity. We're working on an annuity here. So first, we need the rate. So here's the rate. The rate is going to be up top. It's going to be in B four. So here's B for. That's going to be 10 percent. Ten percent is what we have. And then we need the number of periods that's going to be in B, too, which Of course, is three. So and B two.

We have three as a result. And then we have the payments. This is the area that differed when we had the future value of one. We put zero here and then we put the present value of one. The payment means that we're going to have a payment for the annuity that's going to happen. Repeat payments, three payments, in other words, of 100 dollars in this case. So if we put an item here and we put a number of periods, the system is saying, oh, you're talking about an annuity that has three items, three payments. So that's what we have. Hundred dollars in the payment. That gives us the answer of the three thirty one. It's negative because that's typically the way the system will produce the answer.

We could put a negative in front of it if we want to flip the side, as we'll see in the next chapter. Here's the actual formula that we're looking at. We could also enter into an excel in this format equals negative. I put negative just to flip the side, to make it a positive number, AFV future value brackets. And then we're looking for the rate. The rate is F to be four. So here's B, here's four. So that's 10 percent. And then we have KOMMA to go to the next function. Number of periods, that is BE2. So B two, which Of course is three. And so there we have that and then commonly go to the next function. And then we have the payments, the payment, not this one or on the payment. So the payment is a B three, B three, which is a hundred dollars. These two are not required.

So we don't need to add anything to those items. This is all we need for the annuity. And again, this last one is kind of a tricky one. We had a present value of one, this would be zero. If we're talking about an annuity as we are here and a future value of one, this would be zero. If we have a future value annuity, as we do here, then we're going to be using the amount of the one hundred dollars in the payment amount. Remember that we can use this goal, seek features if we need to search for or find some other variable that is within. The future value of an annuity type calculation.

So, for example, if we wanted to find the rate or if we wanted to find the periods and we knew all other information, we don't really need to look for and find and know how to have a separate type of formula within Excel and memorize three different types of formulas. We can use the future value and we could use a goal, seeking to figure out what the missing value is. So in other words, we can use the future value formula here. And we could use Excel to say, I know what this answer is. Would you please tell me what the rate is given this information? And by doing that, we don't need a separate function up here.

We can use the future value to figure out what the rate should be. The same with the periods. The point and if you want to look at that, will have Excel sheets and we'll work through that in Excel to show how that is done. The point here is that we can really get a lot out of just knowing the present value formula, the future value formula that gives us the present value of one, the present value of an annuity, future value of one, future value of an annuity, and the ability to look at these other items. The number, the rate and the number of periods as the unknown. If that is the situation we're looking for as well. So we can do a lot with really just knowing those two main core functions, the present value within Excel and the future value within Excel.

Future Value Annuity Months

In this chapter, we will take a look at the future value of an annuity calculation, this time using months as the period as opposed to years as the period, who's going to be our information up top? We have the number of months, the number of periods being months, this time three periods once again. That being the big change here, those three periods, not years. Now, in terms of months, the payments are going to be 10000. The rate is going to be 12 percent. We can do this three ways. We can do that with the formula, with the use of tables, with the use of Excel. We're going to be concentrating on the tables and excel at the table to the right, as we can see, have the rate up to the periods to the left side.

Neither the rate nor the periods show what periods we're talking about. Are we talking about the rate per year? Per month? What's going to be the period? As long as we use the same period for both the period column and the rate, then we'll be OK. So what we need to do then is change the rate over here from a yearly rate to a monthly rate. Note that within a book problem and in practice, you're generally not given oftentimes the monthly rate. And if it is given, it'll say per month, because if it doesn't say anything, it's assumed it will be the yearly rate, because that's normally the rate we just assumed to have. So normally we'll have to take a yearly rate and say, OK, let's break it down into a monthly amount.

To do that, we're going to take the 12 percent, divide it by 12. Notice, that's an even calculation here to give us the one percent. And that's because, Of course, if we're forced to use the tables, we need something that's even that will fit within the table. So we need a percentage that we have up top within the tables in practice. We may have fractions and we're OK with that. That means that book problems oftentimes will not have monthly periods, but only yearly periods in practice. We may have to deal with, Of course, monthly periods as well. So keep that in mind. We're at one percent per month, and then we just choose the number of months, which in our case is going to be three that gives us the three points oh three oh one.

So we've got the payments, 10000. We've got the amount three point oh three oh one about giving us the future value of the annuity of thirty thousand three one. Then if we take a look at our functions within Excel, we can do this with a function within Excel. So here it's going to be our argument. Here's their future value up top. We're going to put this into our argument area. So we have the rate in the top box, which is going to be four. So B four is here. We have the 12 percent and B four key points here. We're going to take that and divide it by 12. So we're going to take the yearly rate divided by 12, giving us the monthly rate. In that case, it wouldn't matter and excel if this was something other than 12 percent, if it was like, you know, five percent divided by 12, we'd get some small number here.

That's OK. Excel can deal with that. In our case, it's coming out to be one percent point zero one. And then we got the number of periods B to that and so be two, three periods of those periods representing months. Now, how do we know that? Because we're using a monthly rate and therefore the periods will be coinciding with that and B per month. There are three on the right. Then the payment is in B three. So within B three, we have ten thousand, that being the payment that's going to produce the answer of thirty thousand three or one. It's a negative here if we want to flip the sign.

Once we have generated the formula, we can put a negative in front of the function that will flip the sign, in essence, taking that number and multiplying at times the negative one. So we have equal negative future value and then we have before. So before it's going to be the B for the rate divided by 12, the number of periods comma, and then B two. So within B two, we have the number of periods, which is going to be three. And then comma, next argument be three, which is the payment amount. This being an annuity. We have the payment, which is going to be 10,000.

Present Value Cash Flow Examples

In this chapter, we will take a look at an example of the present value of cash flows for a capital investment. Here is our data set. We're going to have a rate of 12 percent. We have our year zero through five years. We're going to say that our cash flow is going to start off with a negative cash flow as if we have an investment. So this would be the initial investment, that cash flow being negative. And then we have the cash flows, positive portions. You're one, two, three and four. Forty thousand. That's going to be the return on the investment or positive cash flows from the investment. And then you're five seventy thousand the seventy thousand, including forty thousand for the return, as well as a salvage value for it. We're going to say we're selling the equipment at the end for the difference.

That being the thirty thousand. When we consider a data set such as this, the question is, how are we going to present value this? What we would like to do is take all of this information and pull it back to the current currency so we can measure all of this information, all these different dollar amounts in terms of the same measurement, in terms of time period. As of today, the present time period, time period zero. Now, there's a couple of ways that we can do this within the present value type of calculations. One, we could present value each year. I can look at each year and say, hey, look, these years are different. The cash flows are different. Any time that is the case, then I'll just take the cash flows for each year, use the present value of one as opposed to the present value of an annuity for each year.

And that and then add those together that will give us the present value. That's going to be one approach. Actually, a very effective approach if we have something like Excel also gives us more detail than another type of approach or other types of approaches would. However, if we're doing this by hand, then, Of course, calculating the present value of each year can be a little bit cumbersome if we're doing it in Excel. Not very difficult at all. We can do that quite quickly. And it might be the best way to go because it does give us more information. What we can also do is say, OK, can I break this out into a shorter type of calculation in some format so we could look for an annuity type of calculator in this data set, for example, we can see these items are an annuity.

So we've got one, two, three and four. They are going to be in the format of an annuity. We have the same payments, the same time periods. We could even extend it to year five and say there's forty thousand. That's an annuity payment. And in the 30000 is going to be over and above that that we can calculate as a single sum. So that's one way we can approach this data. We could say, how can we minimize the calculations that we need? Well, we can take the first year or the year zero as a different data set. It is what it is, because it is as of this point in time, it's the one hundred and fifty thousand. We could take the one through four and think of it as an annuity. Calculating it with an annuity type of format.

And then we can take year five and we can calculate the present value of one. That's one way we can break this out. If we take a look at that, we can say, all right, with year zero and it is what it is. It's one hundred and fifty thousand. That's going to be the initial outlay. It is what it is, because as of this point in time, we don't need to present value it. It is at the present value. And then we could take a look, take a look at year five, year five be the other year that we're going have to break out separately and present your five present values, year five back to the current time period. We're not going to go through the present value calculations here. We're going to go through the approach with this chapter.

Remember, we could calculate it three different ways. We're using the present value of one. We could do that with a formula. We could do that with the use of tables, or we could do that in Excel. If we were to use Excel, that would be the easiest way to do it, the most efficient way to do it. We'll have an Excel example problem to go and show those calculations as well. But you could test any of those ways if you so choose. We run the present value for year five, bringing it back to year zero. That gives us thirty nine thousand seven hundred and twenty. And then we can think of these items one through four as annuities. So we can calculate it as an annuity. Again, there's three ways we could do it.

We can use the annuity formula. We can use the annuity tables, present value annuity tables, or we can use Excel and just do one calculation for these time periods of time periods, one through four. Then we can have one calculation that will take all those back to the present value because they have an annuity. And then if we were to sum that up, then we're going to say that the present value is 11000 to 14. The cash flow is eighty thousand. In other words, if we were just to take the cash flow. Eighty thousand if we discount it at 12 percent. We're going to say that the present value is going to be eleven thousand two hundred and fourteen.

This is one way to manage the data. When you see the data, you want to be able to visualize how you want to manage the data, when you see the data and someone else giving you that information. You want to be able to look at it and say, OK, I see what they did. I see how they organize their table and go from there. This type of calculation is going to be that one that has the least amount of calculations to it. So it gets to the bottom line, 11 to 14 in the quickest fashion, but it also provides the least amount of detail. And if you're using Excel, it's pretty easy to add a little bit more detail, which most people I would typically prefer, if you're presenting data to somebody that just wants the bottom line and wants to see as few numbers as possible.

Then this one might be a good approach. If you're talking to somebody that wants a little bit more detail, possibly see the cash flow and the present value per year, then we might want to take a different approach. Here's another way that we could format the same data. You'll see that we have the year's up top. So a year zero, one, two, three, four and five and then the total. And what we're going to do now is not worry about the fact that there's an annuity. We could say there's an annuity in there, but I'd rather just present the value each year because that's going to give us a better visual of what is going on. So, in other words, the annuity is great to kind of compact the information down. And if you're talking about an annuity kind of situation, you may want to run that calculation for , for quickness.

However, if you're talking about a capital project, you may want to give more detail for it so they can have more detail for the decision making process that usually involves having the payments broken out and this way in this format. You can have very complex kinds of payments that will be broken out as long as you can group them into the proper year. And then we can basically present value each year fairly easily with the use of Excel. So in this case, we all would do and say, all right, here's the cash flows, I'm breaking them out, just here's our cash flows. One, fifty, forty, forty, forty, forty, and then seventy. And you're five. And then we would just present value each year. So each year we're just going to present value. You're zero is going to be one hundred and fifty. And then we're going to run the present value of one calculation.

We don't need a calculation here because it is what it is. Year one through five, we're going to use the present value of one again. Could use a formula to do that. We could use tables to do that. We could use Excel, which I would prefer to do if we had Excel. This will be a fairly easy calculation we can do. We can auto fill it using the same formatting to copy the formula in a similar way that we can copy over some function as well. So to do that, we can get these numbers, then we'll present values again each year. So we're not using an annuity in this case. We're just going to present value each year and then add that up. We get our same 11000 to 14. So you might see the data that is going to be formatted this way.

This might be a good way to present the data, because it gives you that bit more detail. It gives you the cash flow per year. Now, we might want even more detail than that. We could break this out in a more detailed type of way. We could say, OK, let's have the year zero through five and the total. And then we're also going to break out the type of information on the left hand side. So we can say, hey, this is the investment. It happened in year zero. I'm going to break that out separately. That's the investment in year zero. Here's the total investment. It's a negative number. Here's the cash received in investment. So these are going to be that cash inflows that we got forty thousand forty thousand forty thousand forty thousand. And I'm going to include the forty thousand in year five because of this.

Seventy forty of it was the same 40 as the prior year. Thirty of it is salvage value. So then we can break out the salvage value and say that happened in year five and then we can have our totals, this total column then being the same as basically what we had up here. So the same thing. We're just got the total column. However, this format breaks out, the investment cash received salvage before getting to that total, providing us with a little bit more detail. So, again, if we want to present this to somebody, we can provide a bit more detail. If we break it out in this format, then we'll present value in the same way we did before. We're going to say present value. The 150 is just a 150 because it's in your zero, the present value of one through five.

We're then going to use the present value of one where we can use the formula, we can use the tables, we can use excel. I would prefer to use Excel. We then get the 11 to 14. This is a nice way to see it, because, again, you get this is the initial investment. We get broken out. We could see the cash flows that are not present valued, the total cash flows, and then we can see the present value calculations and we can see them, Of course, per year. Another way we might organize this data is in more of a vertical type scenario. And this is what I would tend to prefer. I would tend to. With the data in this type of format, so a more vertical format, we would say, then we're going to have the years running down on the column and then we're going to have the cash flows right next to it.

So this is going to be a compact, more summarized type of format, basically just picking up the data. Same format as it's shown in our data set years one through five, and then the cash flows for years, one through five. And then we can calculate the present value to the right in a column format. So we're going to say here's the present value of your zero. Once again, the one hundred and fifty thousand and then will present value each year. So we're going to present value each year using one of our methods. Either we use the formulas or the tables or we use Excel. We would prefer to use Excel and then we can sum them up in this fashion. So this gives us, again, a little bit more detail.

We're not breaking out the categories as we'll see next time in more of a vertical fashion. But it's going to give us the cash flows per year and the present value of those cash flows per year. And again, we could copy the present value formula down using an autofill function, copying the formula which can make this table fairly easy. We could do this fairly quickly once we're able to visualize what the table should look like. And then lastly, we can add some more detail with this vertical type of format where the years are in the columns, this gets a little bit more tricky because the headers we're going to have to add more detail in the headers.

So we're going to need more space or we're going to need to shorten the headers. But I tend to prefer this kind of vertical format as opposed to us listing out in a horizontal or in the columns or in the row. In other words, here's the same table in terms of the rows where we broke out the details. We have a little bit more room to enter all the data into all the text here as opposed to us. If we flip these and put the text on top and the numbers to the left. Then we have to fix the text into a smaller space, which can take a little bit more time. But I think it's an easier way to see it in more of a vertical format. So that's what we'll work on now. The same type of chart, same type of detail. But now just flipping the X and Y axis is.

So we'll have year one, two, three, four and five. We're going to start with the initial investment. So initial investment up top is in year zero, and then there's the total year zero. Then we're going to say cash received in investment four years, one through five, just like we saw when we saw it in the rose is going to be two hundred thousand. And then we're going to these salvage because remember, the seventy thousand includes salvage value, so 40 plus the 30 salvage. So there's the total salvage. And if we total this up, then we're going to total them across this way. 150, forty, forty, forty, forty. And there's the 70. We end up with our cash flows.

Now, we're at the same point here that we were when we saw the prior chapter or the prior chapter where we just had basically the cash flows. We got a little bit more detail. We can see the cash flows for different categories, investments, the receipt of cash and the salvage. Then we'll practice or then we'll calculate the present value, present value per year and year zero. It is what it is, the one hundred and fifty. And then we'll use the calculations for years, one through five. We can do them three different ways. We can use the formulas, we can use the tables, we can use Excel. I would prefer to use Excel and get down to that 11 to 14. This is typically the way I would generally do it.

I think this is the easiest way to see it, although it can be a little bit difficult to see the groupings of the headers up top as opposed to if you put them in the horizontal, where it can be a little bit easier to fit that. Just note, however, that you may see all of these different types of formats, all of these different types of tables within a chapter. And when you see different types of tables, you start to think that there's a whole different data set or there's this is a different thing, a whole different animal. It's not these are just different ways for us to group the same information. Once you're able to visualize how this information can be grouped in different ways, it's far less confusing to deal with and work with.

Future Value Cash Flow Examples

In this chapter, we will take a look at an example of cash flows and the calculation of future value with those cash flows will take both a look at annuity, cash flows, future value of an annuity, future value of a single sum with these cash flows. We're taking a look at the flows to the left. Our rate is going to be 14 percent, and then we're going to have our years zero one, two, three, four, five. And then our cash flow is 30000, 5000, 5000, 5000, eight thousand ten thousand sixty three thousand. What we want to get good at is taking a look at the numbers that we're using. What we're trying to do for future value. We want to get an idea of what we're future value in and then take an approach on how we're going to future value it.

So in this case, one, we're doing the future value, meaning we're going to have a value at the end of this cash flow period. Usually when people think about a future value, if you want to apply a scenario, the scenario to apply is usually an investment type of activity for the future value. In other words, if we were to put money into an investment, that would then be generating a return on it. Then at the end of the investment, we would have how much money is there at the end of the investment? Now, that could be a little bit confusing, because when we think of future value in time, value of money, we might be thinking about just the value of the dollar. And when we think about it in terms of an investment, obviously, we're thinking about the return on the investment, the rate.

We're thinking about the return on the investment. So remember that we can't think of the future value in terms of the time value of money. In other words, the decline in the value of money due to something like inflation. And think about the future value then has to be something higher than the present value. And Of course, if we think about opportunity costs in terms of the future value and investment in the future value, then we can think about the rate of return or the interest rate or the rate of return. We're going to get on the investment. And in the future, value is going to be representing the future value as we get to that future value. When we think about these investments, Of course, it will be valued in absolute dollar terms, the dollars at that future time period.

And Of course, that future time period, dollar amount when we think of it in terms of the value. With regard to the same amount today, it's going to be a higher dollar amount in the future than the same value today in terms of purchasing power. And in terms of the investment or rate of return we could get today. So that's going to be the thought process. We're thinking you probably want to think, all right, this looks kind of like an investment. We are going to be looking at these cash flows. We've got a 14 percent return. We got sixty three thousand. If we add up the cash flows, it's going to be higher than that. Given the fact that these are going to be basically earning or going up due to the investment or the future value, then being higher than the original investment that that we're putting in, which is going to be these the cash flows. And we would then say, all right, these aren't even payments, so we can't just use an annuity formula.

That's the first thing we would think. Well, could I do this with one easy calculation with just an annuity formula? No, because the payments are not all the same. So we've got thirty thousand beginning five thousand five thousand five thousand eight thousand ten thousand. So that's the first thing we're going to say. I can't just do one calculation then. Well, we could break it out and this is what we can always do. We can break it out to each individual a year and do a future value calculation for each individual year. And that might be worth doing. We'll take a look at that approach, or we might try to consolidate our information down and break it out in some other way. For example, we might say, well, you know, each year, one through five have a five thousand component in it.

We could use an annuity calculation to calculate the five thousand components and then do another calculation for the added amounts. Four years, four and your five. So that's the shortest amount of like numbers we can present with. So let's do that first. Also note that when you see this type of investment, this would be a common type of investment where we would have an original amount of thirty thousand, and then we would have some amount that we would be putting in each year annually. And then think about, OK, what would the total be at the end of that time period? The future value. So we can say, all right, you're zero is going to be fifty seven thousand seven hundred and sixty two.

Now, we're not going to go through all the calculations here. Remember, we can do that three different ways. We can do that with formulas that we can do with the use of tables or we can do that with Excel. What we want to do here is look at the grouping. How are we going to group this information? So we're going to assume we use either of those three ways. I would use Excel to do that and say that we need to future value the 30000, the number of periods being the five periods, and we get the fifty seven thousand seven sixty two. We had to do the future value of one there because we're not including this in our annuity. And then one through five, we're going to say there is a 5000 component in years, one through five.

Therefore, although four and five have more than 5000 in it, we're just going to account for the 5000 part of it and four and five to make it for us to use an annuity formula. And that would give us thirty three fifty one. So we're going to take the annuity future value of an annuity. Five periods. Five thousand is the amount. And then we can just take it. All right. Now, there's the difference in your form, which is going to be the eight thousand minus the five thousand. It's going to be three thousand. And we're going to have to take the future value of one to calculate for the three thousand four hundred and twenty.

We'll get a little bit more detail in the calculations in the second example, and then we can go to your five, say, five thousand minus five thousand or the added 5000 is going to be what we calculate here. We could do the future value of the future value of the amount we don't need to. However, here, because it's the last year, so it's not as if this was put in at the end of year five, it's not going to be growing any time then it's been put in at the end of the year. And then if we add those up, we're going to say that total then ninety nine to thirty three. So here's our total cash flow. What we put in here is the present value of or the future value of the annuity. That's one way we can break this out. And it shows less calculations gets to the bottom line a bit more directly. But it's also a little bit more confusing.

So if you're dealing with someone that just wants to see the bottom line and they don't really care about the calculations, they just want to see the bottom line, then this might be the easiest way to show it, to give that bottom line. However, if we want to see more data and want to give some understanding on the calculation, it might just be the easiest thing to do for future value. Each one of the years. So another way we can format this data, say, all right, let's take the number of years then. And typically, oftentimes a nice little trick with an excel is to then reverse the number of years. So the number of years being zero through five. Let's reverse it five through zero. That helps us to enter formulas into Excel. And we can then autofill the formulas down much more easily by using this method.

And then we can enter the cash flows. So here's our cash flows directly, which is going to future value each year. Then we can go ahead and future value each year and do the future value of one not using an annuity. So obviously, the first one, we're going to future value the thirty thousand, we're going to use two years of five years rather than zero, as we would with the present value. So it's the reverse. And that's why it's nice to have the years reversed up here that allows us to pull up this information instead of reaching down here to pick up this number five in the formula. If you want to see more detail on this, we'll show an Excel example on it so you can see why this helps. It's easier.

And then we're going to have the five thousand again. We're going to pick up the period of four. And that will be future value over the four periods, eight thousand four, forty five. Then we have the five thousand over three periods as future valued at seven four 08. Then the five thousand futures are valued at two periods, four, six, four, nine four. And then we have the eight thousand future values in one period. Nine one two zero. And finally the 10000 thousand has no future value. It is what it is at the end of that five year period adding those up that gives us our ninety nine to 33. So there's just a few different ways that we can see this data.

Once we understand the future value formulas and we understand an annuity and a future value of one, our main goal then is to say, OK, here's our data. How do I want to format this data to make it easiest to calculate and best to look at? Oftentimes, if we have an annuity involved, that'll be the easiest calculation. But even then, it may not give the amount of data that we want, even if this was a straight annuity. Sometimes it's nice to actually break out each year, the future value of each year, the cash flow of each year, because then we get to see some detail for each of those years.

Present Value Terms Used In Capital Budgeting

In this chapter, we will take a look at present value terms used in capital budgeting. Our goal here is to understand the relationship between these terms so that when we see these different types of terms, we're not intimidated. We don't think this is going to be a completely new concept that we have to learn. Typically, these terms will be related to the same ideas of present value. If we understand present value, then we can understand these new terms with a little bit more information. These terms will usually be based around the interest rate. So the interest rate that we are using can be a little bit confusing. We might call it different things and we might think about how we got to that rate in different ways.

Once we've determined that rate, however, usually we're going to be applying the present value concepts in a similar fashion. Once we know how to apply the concepts, how to apply the calculations, then we could use the rate that is given. The first idea we think about with regard to the time value of money is that the future dollars are going to be worth less than the current dollars, and that typically is due to inflation. Inflation causes the purchasing power of the money to go down. A typical inflation rate is usually between one and five percent in the US. The rate that we use to discount them might be something that's going to be close to what we believe the rate of inflation will be.

So if we have this series of payments and we want to bring them all back to year zero at this point in time, then we might use a rate that we think is going to approximate the interest rate. And that would be approximating the time value of money or the loss in purchasing value due to inflation. So we might call this a discount rate, but we might set the rate to what we think a reasonable rate of inflation will be in order to discount cash flow payments to get them back to current value dollars. So that's one method that we can use. Now, we could also use a discount rate that's going to be based on not only the purchasing power of the dollar going down, but on opportunity cost.

So in other words, we might say, hey, where could I put my money if I wasn't to invest it in this project? If I had this one hundred and eighty thousand dollars, where could I put it if I wasn't to invest it here? Well, we know we could at least put it in the bank if we think that we could put it in the bank or some other investment. That being the opportunity, cost and gain, say, eight percent on the bank, then we might say, hey, I need to set this rate to be high enough that it's going to be higher than what I could get elsewhere. So we might set this rate a little bit higher. We may still call it a discount rate, but we're not setting it at the rate of inflation just to see the decrease in the purchasing power of money.

We're now setting it at the opportunity cost, the cost that we can invest in something else and get basically a return in some other place. So in this format, you might call this a hurdle rate, some rate that we want to clear, we want to get over this rate. We're going to say this is the minimum rate or the required return on investment is another term that this might be called. We will do the present value calculation in much the same way or pretty much exactly the same way with a different discount rate. But the discount rate represents something different. It doesn't represent the value of the dollar going down due to inflation. It now represents the opportunity cost of some other investment that we could be investing in.

And therefore, if we were to present this series of payments with something like a hurdle rate, then anything that comes out positive means that the cash flows are above that rate of return and therefore would be something that would clear that test and possibly be something that we would want to invest in. The third concept that we often see is the internal rate of return, the IRR. Now, this is going to be more difficult to calculate mathematically, very easy to do with something like Excel. But the concept is easy to understand once we understand the present value. So the internal rate of return is the rate at which the net present value is zero.

So in other words, if we were to pick an interest rate or a discount rate at which this flow, this series of payments would be zero, that would be the internal rate of return. So let's take a look at some examples. This one can be the most abstract to think about, but conceptually becomes clear with example. So let's say this is our cash flow information and we group that information. Our initial investment is one hundred and eighty thousand. We have the sixty thousand each year of the receipts that will happen after that initial investment. And then the salvage value is going to be the sixty thousand minus the ninety thousand or the 30000 is going to be the salvage. So the sixty in the thirty is that ninety. Here's our total cash flows.

These, in essence, just match our cash flows up top. If we were to present this with five percent, we're not going to go through the calculations here. You could use a table, you could use the formulas or you could use Excel. We're going to go over the concepts here. We do use and calculate this in Excel if you want to take a look at that example problem. Then we would present value this and we come up to the. One of three to 74. Now, remember that this five percent we're thinking is basically close to inflation. The close to the decline in the value of the dollar. So we're basically taking this cash flow and bringing it back to year zero dollars in terms of purchasing power. Is the concept of using something like five percent, three to five in the U.S.

would be somewhere around what inflation would be. Now, let's do the same type of cash flows. We have the same cash flows here, but now we're going to be basing it on 10 percent. And this is something we might call a hurdle rate. This might be based on the opportunity cost of our next best investment. In other words, we need to get our return higher than 10 percent in order to accept the project. So that means that if we present the value using 10 percent, we're going to do the same calculations. It's not something different. It's not a completely different animal. It's the same type of calculation. It's just that now this 10 percent represents the investment that we want to have. This is our required return on investment for us to take the project.

And we are hitting that required return on investment any time we present value, calculate net present value using that rate and we come up with a positive number. So if this was one, it would be acceptable because we would be clearing that 10 percent. So that's going to be the key concept there. Now, we can think about the internal rate of return. You can think about this same series of numbers. And we want to take a look at the internal rate of return. All that means is that we want to set, we want to figure out what this rate would be so that this present value series of numbers would end up to be zero. So we want to be able to present a value that is zero.

Normally we know the rate and then we present value and we see what we get. In this case, we want to basically set the present value to zero and determine what the rate is. Now, again, that's a little bit more difficult to do mathematically. Very easy to do with Excel. And conceptually, it makes perfect sense. We're going to say, OK, well, I need to know what the rate is in order to get the present value to zero. That's going to be the internal rate of return. Twenty three in this case. So just realize that the internal rate of return isn't different. It's just kind of the reverse type of calculation. You could do this type of calculation with, in essence, trial and error. You could just basically pick a number, calculate the present value, and then just keep changing this number until it becomes zero.

And Of course, we can use Excel to help us to get this number. We can use a function and excel the IRR equals IRR function, internal rate of return to calculate a series of numbers very easily as well. So once you have an understanding of what this interest rate is, then it could be called different types of things. And at least you know that the calculation is going to be much the same and go through the similar process. And you're not talking about completely different types of things that we're going to go through, although we do want to know what is meant by the interest rate that is set.

Net Present Value Assumptions

In this chapter, we will take a look at some net present value assumptions we want to keep in mind as we apply and use the concepts of net present value. One assumption, it assumes the discount rate is unchanged during the project life. So as we have the project life, we're clearly using one discount rate. And we're assuming, Of course, that the discount rate will be the same unchanged throughout the life of the project. It also assumes that cash flows happen at one point per period as opposed to cash flows happening along or during that time period. So if we were to take a look at an example, the assumption is that the discount rate is something that is going to apply to the life of the project. So if we take a look at this project, we have cash flows from year zero to five.

The initial cash flow happened, the outflow in year zero, one, two, three, four and five being the inflows of forty thousand forty thousand four thousand four thousand and seventy thousand. Then we present the value each year using the same rate. The net present value calculation won't work if we were to use multiple discount rates. If we want to apply a different discount rate to the other three, we typically need to apply the same rate all the way through for the net present value calculation. It also assumes that cash flows happen at one point in time. So if you'll take a look at how these cash flows are working or how we are going to calculate this, we're going to say that the forty thousand, for example, in year one all happened at one point in time so that we can apply the present value type calculation as opposed to it happening throughout the time period.

Therefore, we can apply the present value calculation to one dollar amount and bring that dollar amount back to the present value. And that's what we do for each of the time periods that we can mitigate this to some degree by basically having more time periods. We could break this into a monthly time period if we so choose and try to break out our cash flows on a monthly basis and then present value in the months. But we do have this limitation in that we have to assume when we apply the present value type calculations, that the cash flows all happen at one point in time.

Future Value FV Multiple Forms of Calculation

Corporate finance practices problems within one note for their future value, or AFV, which we're going to calculate in many different ways. One way, including the mathematical formula, a second way, considering the formula that could be calculated in Excel. And a third way, which would be using tables or future value tables to help with the calculation, don't leave profit solely to chance. Instead, use corporate finance. Here we are in one note. If you would like to follow along in one note, you're not required to. But if you have access to it and would like to, we can go into the tab on the left hand side. We're going to be in the practice problems chapter. And then in the problem of the nine one one future value AFV, multiple forms of calculation.

I'll then close this item up so we can be focusing on the practice problem. Our data is going to be up on the left hand side, and then we'll work through that data with basically the blue areas on the bottom. Note our data here. We're typically going to be thinking when we're thinking about future value, kind of like the opposite of the present value. When we're thinking of present value, we're taking something that's going to happen in the future, basically future cash flows, trying to bring that back to the present. Now we're thinking about something that we're putting in place now and thinking about where it will be if we have an investment that will be into the future. So the typical kind of scenario, thinking about, say, investments and like stocks or something, we're going to get a return on it.

We hope we get a return on what kind of return we might get, where we would then be, what the value will be in the future, in the future value using future value, basically dollars at that point in time to do that. We're going to need the amount that we're going to invest. We're going to need the period that we're going to be invested over, which may be determined or given to us in years or months, typically. And then we're going to be needing the percentage of the increase and the compounding of the increase that we believe is going to be taking place. Once we have that, we can then calculate the future value where we expect to be in future value terms at the end of this time period.

So our data is going to be on the left hand side. We're going to invest the ten thousand. The years are going to be the period, three years, and the percentage is going to be the eight percent. We could do this multiple ways and we'll check it out multiple different ways, including our formula, and then we'll think about tables. So the tables that we used in the present value, similar kind of feature, that is a common feature that's going to be used in test problems, because that eliminates kind of like the calculator or the more complex calculator needs that you might have if you have the table. You might also do it with a complex calculator or something like Excel.

So that's the other way that we will consider it in practice. I believe that one of the most efficient ways to use it would be something like Excel to help us with these calculations. Also note that it's useful to break this out, as we'll do in a little bit more detail here to look at it, kind of like a year by year to see what happens from a year to year, because even if you use the math, the formula here then is still kind of a little bit magical. You do the calculation and you get to this magic number at the end. If you actually calculate it with a nearby year or period by period calculation, which is fairly easy to do if you have something like Excel. And I do recommend working on this problem in Excel.

We do have it available. Then you get a bit more understanding of what's going on just from a conceptual basis. So the future value calculation then would be future value equals the present value, which is basically the amount that we're going to be investing. Now, times one plus are the rate of return. In this case, we got eight percent. And then that's going to be the number of periods. In this case, three years. Remember that you want to make sure that you know what type of period you're talking about with regards to the time period, are we talking years? Are we talking about months and so on and so forth. Now, we're going to calculate this one year at a time. So I'm going to do the future value, not for three periods.

First, we'll do it for year one, and then we'll do the same thing for a year or two. And so on. So we'll first use the formula. I'm going to break this formula out into a more like a tax return type of format, write a vertical type of format. And I think this is useful for building things in Excel. If you were to build something in Excel and you wanted to see how it works. It's nice to have this formula broken out from an algebraic type of equation to a table. So I think that's a good thing to work with. And you might want to actually do that in Excel, work through the practice problem in Excel to put that together. Obviously, you can just use the formula, the algebra here as well, and work it through in the algebraic format.

So if I go back up top, I'm going to say the present value is going to be ten thousand. That's going to be what we have up top. There's ten thousand. And then we've got the one plus R to the N that we're going to calculate. So we got this piece that we have, and now I'm going to calculate the second piece in our table here. So the second piece is going to be one which is going to be this one right there. And then we're going to say at the rate we're going to add the rate to, it's a one plus the rate, the rate being eight percent. So one plus the rate would be one hundred and eight percent. So now we've done this entire portion one plus hour, and then we're going to take the number of periods. I'm not taking three in this case. I'm taking one because I'm just looking at one year at this time.

So we're going to consider the one year. That's where that one comes from. One hundred and eight percent. That van is going to give us ten thousand eight hundred, which would make sense if we did the calculation here. Of course, we would take the ten thousand if I'm making eight percent on the year point zero eight. Then we've got the eight hundred plus the original amount of the ten thousand. That would be ten thousand eight. So you could do the same thing by saying

I'm going to multiply this by one hundred and eight percent. So one hundred would be one plus eight percent point zero eight. And so let's do that again.

One plus point zero eight. That would be one oh eight, one hundred and eight percent times the 10000. And that would be ten thousand eight. That's where we would stand then at the end of that time period, that notice that's in future values. When we're considering the future value, we have to consider. What does this percentage mean, this rate means, you know, and we might be considering how we are going to, you know, come up to that rate? Obviously, that's going to be kind of a projected type of thing. Most of the time in terms of what we think the earnings are going to be for a possible type of investment. So then if we go down below, we could do this on a period by period basis and consider this calculation period to period, which can be a little bit. Give us some information.

It's easy to do basically in Excel. So I think it's worthwhile to do in Excel, and it's fairly easy to do a running balanced type of calculation. So we get the ten thousand and then you get the 800. Obviously, the 800 is calculated by the investment of ten thousand times. Do you point to zero eight? There are eight hundred. If you add that to the 10000 plus to ten thousand, that's going to give you that ten thousand eight. Then if you go to year two, then now we're taking that ten thousand eight has now compounded. It's the way we're calculating those rates. Now we got ten thousand eight times two point zero eight percent. That means that the amount of return for year two is eight sixty four.

If I take that eight sixty four plus where we were before ten thousand eight, we then get eleven six, six four. Then if we do that again, we're going to take that amount of times the point zero eight and that's going to give us the nine three three 12. I'm going to add that to the 11 six six four and that's going to give us our 12, 12 five ninety seven. And so then our total of the interest is going to be the total of these over that time period. So note, this is a little less magical. If I was to do the formula for this, I'd still come up with just like the magic endi number, which we'll do later. We only did it for one year before. Later we'll do it for three years to get to that.

Twelve, five, ninety seven. But it's useful to do this if you have Excel. It's quite easy to do this kind of running balance type of formula and get a better perspective of what is happening from period to period. You could do it slightly differently over here. If we took the zero, we got the ten thousand, and then we were just calculating the interest on the right hand side. So now we've got the eight hundred and that brings it up to ten thousand eight. And then once again, we've got the 800 on the right hand side, the eight sixty four on the right hand side to give us the value of the L1 66 for basically the same kind of concept that you can do it a little bit differently or calculate it or do the formula possibly a little bit differently in Excel.

We'll do that more in Excel in our Excel problem. I do recommend working on Excel. Note you can also do this calculation with a calculation in Excel, which would be similar to doing this in a calculator, a financial calculator, as opposed to a normal calculator. And many people will do this, this method. And like the math formula, it kind of magically gives you that end result. It'll magically get you to that end result, which in this case we're using at one period, which will be that ten thousand eight, because we're just using one one year later. But again, if you were to run this and it had multiple periods, it's kind of nice still to put it in Excel and see the details of it, see what the interest difference was going to be from period to period as you think about this. But the formula is going to be something like this. You could do it in an Excel formula like so the present, the future value.

And I'm going to put a negative in front of it. It's going to be brackets. And then you'd find the sales of B three, comma one, comma zero, comma B, one. Again, we'll talk more about this and in Excel when we could see the formulas and the and the relationships of them. But also just realize that when you do that in Excel, you can break this down into basically a function table within Excel, which means it'll give you the rate. So then we would put the rate here in our practice problem, which was eight percent. The number of periods was one. Notice that we're looking at, period. It's here for an entire year. If we were looking at periods that were a month, then we would have to take the rate divided by 12. The period has to equal the rate amount.

We usually think of rates in terms of years. And so if we're talking about a period of something other than a year, such as a month, we've got to make sure that we break down the rate to be relative to that by taking the yearly rate, which is typically given. And in that case, divided by 12. But we're talking the yearly rates here. So we just take the rate and then the payment amount. We're not making payment amounts. That would be if we had an annuity type of calculation, multiple payments. Thinking about considering multiple investments, which we may talk about in the future. But here we're just going to put a zero there. And that's why we could use the same function for both Excel and for.

I'm sorry for the two calculations for the future value of an annuity and the future value of one, which typically with annuity tables or with the tables, you need to separate tables with Excel. You can use the same formula, in essence, a future value formula, because you could put basically a zero on the payment here and then use this one, which would not be required if it were an annuity, but is required if its present value is one. And that would be one or the present value or the amount of the investment of the 10000. And that will give us our calculation here, which you could see as the ten thousand eight hundred on the calculation. Notice that if you get good at this, you stop using this table and they give you this little thing down at the bottom when you start to enter the formula.

And that's usually a lot faster. And you can use that once you get good at the investment. You get the rate of the comma, the number of periods, the comma, and then the payments, which is zero, you can see here. And then the present value, which we pick up the present value in the cells. So then we have the table for the future value of one. We can also do this using the tables. So here's the tables down below. As you do the tables, you've got to make sure you're picking up the proper table, which is part of the problem. Oftentimes when you're doing this in like a book problem for a test or something like that, because there's present value tables. If I was trying to take the future period back, there's present value annuity tables. There's future values of annuity and there's future values of a single component. So you want to make sure that you're picking up the proper table.

Once you have the proper table, then you can basically say, OK, I'm going to take the amount, the 10000 times the amount that I'm getting from the table, which would be based on the percent and the periods. Once again, be careful if you're talking about periods and months or years here. We're talking years. And I'm not looking at the three years, just the one year we'll start off with and then we'll add one year at a time. So eight percent one year is going to be that one point zero eight. There's one point or eight once again, getting us to that ten thousand eight hundred for that one year time period. So multiple methods to get to the same spot. If you're talking to different people and they're using different methods, make sure that you realize they're doing the same thing.

They're just doing a different method. And many people only have one method in their mind, you know. So if you do something different or you try to talk to them differently about it, they're not going to know what you're talking about. So you got to know what they're talking about by knowing that whatever they're doing is just one method of doing the same thing here. So let's do a similar type of thing for two years now. So we'll do the formula for two years. Here's our formula, same formula. But now we're going to say two of the three years have passed present values, the 10000. Then we'll calculate this. Enter part one plus R to the end, which is going to be one plus the rate of eight percent, giving us that one hundred and eight percent. Now to N, which is now two years. Here's the different factor.

It's two. So if we do this calculation and I change the calculator up top to a scientific calculator, so if you use a Windows program, that should have a scientific calculator so I can take it to the power of two. We do have a power of two here, but I'd like to be able to do two to three next time. So I'm going to go ahead and take the scientific calculator out to do so. So once again, we have one plus the point zero eight, and then we're going to say that's going to equal the one point zero eight. And then I'm going to take that. I'm going to instead of hitting this one, but instead I'm going to hit this item down here, and then that puts a little carrot up top to the power of two.

And that's going to give us then our one one six point six four, and then I'll take that ten thousand and that'll give us R six, six, four. So that would be after the two time periods in this case, those time periods being in years. Once again, if we did this in our little calculation here, we got the ten thousand plus eight percent we saw before would be the eight hundred now with a ten thousand eight after year one. Now it's year two. We have in that ten thousand eight times the eight sixty four that gives us to our 11 six six four that matches our 11 six six four up here. So note you can do this run in the table down here in Excel, which again I think is useful to do. You can look at it in that format or in this format.

So then scrolling down, the next thing we could do, we could do this with Excel, which is similar to a financial calculator, which should get us once again magically to that end result. You could see it in this format, which would be the rate, the rate being in the eight percent. And then the number of periods this time I'm taking two of the three years, comma zero, which is the number of payments, because we're not making payments. We're saying this is going to be just a future value of one. And then we're going to take the present value, which is ten thousand. And that would then give us once again our end result, in essence, being that 11, six, six, four. So then we have the future value tables that we could use.

So a future value table, same calculation for two periods. Now we take that 10000 times the amount from the table, making sure we have the proper table, the future value of one table. And now we're looking at that eight percent, making sure that when we're looking at the period side of things, we got the proper period. In this case being years. So two years. And we have two percent for two years. And that's going to give us the one point one six, six, four. So one point one six, six four here, ten thousand times. The one point one six six four gives us the 11, six, six, four, 11, six six for matching what we have up top 11, six, six, four, and the 11, six, six, four. Note that the tables could be off a little bit because this ratio or this number might be rounded.

So you could be off a little bit by the different use of these methods. The math would be the most accurate as long as you're rounding or full or not rounding all the calculations as you go through when you use the table, you're going around. If you do this in Excel, Excel well, not round. If you're using ratios, even though it'll look like it's rounded because it won't show all of the decimal points in the number. For example, it might cut this off to like two decimals, even though it's the full number that you're using to calculate. So be careful of rounding with these kinds of calculations. So next, we have three years. Let's do the same thing for three years now.

The full thing now, we got a three year investment. Present value is going to be ten thousand. Now we're going to do this inner part, which is going to be then the one plus the eight percent. There's one hundred and eight percent. Now we have the power of three this time. So if we do that quick calculation, we've got, OK, scientific calculators, what we need now. I'm not as used to one and then I'm going to say plus two point zero eight. And then I'm going to take that and say, now we got the one oh eight. I'm going to take that to the power with a little care, come up here, a little carrot of three. And that's going to be if we move the decimal point over one to five point nine, seven percent or one point two nine five nine seven one, two, so on.

And if we take that ten thousand, we're going to get twelve, five, nine, seven. So note that twelve, five, nine, seven. If I was to build my table like you might ask, where do they get the future value table? If I took that number and divided it by the 10000, that's going to give us our one point two five nine seven one two, which should be, I believe, the amount that would be on the future value table, which will take a look shortly. So then if I go back down, we're going to say now, if I did this in terms of Excel, which would be similar to a financial calculator we would take, then the the the the I believe the first one is the rate. I don't have the little description here, the rate. And then comma, we would then have, I believe, the number of periods which in this case would be three.

And then the payments, which is zero, which you can reflect by having instead of a zero, just two commas, which would then take you to the present value, which I believe is the ten thousand once again, calculating the same amount. We can use the tables then, which was let's just delete this ten thousand times the rate that rate one point twenty five, nine, seven. Close to the rate we got up here, one point two five nine seven one two. So notice the table is going to round it down to how many decimals? Four decimals. So the will could or could be around indifference. So same thing here. We got the interest rate. Make sure you're lining up the interest rate with the periods. So the periods happened to be years. These rates then will be, you know, the rate per period. In this case, years.

So we got the eight and then here's the amount for three years. That's the one point two, five, nine, seven. There's one point two, five, nine, seven, ten thousand times that. One point two, five, nine, seven. That gives us our twelve thousand five ninety seven. That amount should match or be close to the twelve thousand five ninety seven here, although it doesn't match perfectly because the tables are rounded. So actually, the calculation up here, if you did it in Excel or something like that, because you're not rounding the decimals in Excel or using a formula will actually be a little bit more exact, which may not make a difference for Decision-Making purposes, but could make a difference for practice problem or test questions or things like that. So.

Want to be careful and make sure that you're using the method. It also could be a point of differentiation. If, for example, the book is trying to get you to use the tables and try not to get you to use the calculator, then they may put that difference in. They may say this is the right answer, because if you choose the other one, which is more exact, actually, that means you must have used another method to get to that answer so they can try to force you not to use another method by making you, you know, putting the answers related to the difference in rounding so that they can kind of force you to use the method that they told you to use within it.

Present Value (PV) Calculation – Multiple Ways

Corporate finance practice problem in one note. We're going to do the present value calculation, PVG calculation. We will do so multiple different ways, including a mathematical formula, looking at the function of the formula within an Excel type of calculation, as well as using tables. Get ready. It's time to achieve corporate financial finesse with corporate finance. Here we are in our practice problem. In one note, if you would like to follow along, you're not required to. But if you have access to one to one notes, and we'd like you to , I'm going to open up this tab on the left hand side in the practice problems chapter. We're down here on the nine 12 present value calculation multiple ways. I'm then going to close this item up and we'll go through our practice problem.

We have the data up top. We're going to use that data to do our calculation, calculating in multiple different ways, including the actual math calculation that we will be doing. Then we have the Excel tables, which is similar to our use of Excel formulas, which is similar to a financial calculator. Then we will use tables. The mathematical formula is useful to know. So you understand the math. It's also something that possibly will be there in book problems and calculation in Excel or a financial calculator, probably more common in practice, probably a good tool to have and to know in practice and in the tables. Also a good tool to have and know, because it could be a simplified way to do the math. And it's often used in practice problems as well for schools, because, again, you can eliminate the financial calculator by doing that.

OK, so we had the receipt. We have to receive it in the future. So we have the future values going to be ten thousand. We're going to get ten thousand in the future. You could think about a situation where like, you know, we're going to get a payment that's going to happen at some time in the future, or possibly we owe something at some point in time in the future. At that point in time, the future is going to be 12 years as we think of the periods in the future. You've got to make sure that you understand the periods as either be in years or months or whatever the period is going to be that you're going to be calculating in. And then the discount rate, which is something that we would have to figure and we take into consideration things like inflation and other types of factors that could be involved for the discount rate.

Once we have that, then we can do our present value calculation. We'll start it off with a formula present value equal in the future value, which is at ten thousand times one over one plus the rate being five percent here to the in a number of periods, in our case years that the. Well, we're going to break this formula down into a kind of a vertical type of calculation. Really good practice to do so, because you could put that vertical calculation in something like an Excel file and have a good worksheet with it. I think it's easier for a lot of people to actually break down that way. So you can do it algebraically here, plug this information into the formula, or break a formula like this up into some kind of table, which I think is useful to do. So let's see what that will look like. We've got the future value is going to be ten thousand.

So that's going to be at this point, the ten thousand ten thousand here. Then we're going to be calculating this part of the formula, which is going to be one plus hour to the in periods. So I'm going to do that calculation here and we're going to have the one. So this is going to be the one. And then we're going to say the rate is going to be five percent. So that one plus the five percent, that, Of course, is going to give us the one hundred and five percent. One hundred and five percent. Then we have the number up, period. So we're going to take this then to end that period thing. Twelve now. And that's going to give us then this one point seven nine five, eight, six. Now, if you do this in a calculator, you kind of need a scientific calculator, one that you can take to the power of something other than squared.

So I'm going to pick the scientific calculator here and I'm going to take the one, say the one plus the point zero five, that's going to be one hundred and five percent to the power of twelve. And that's why you got to use this scientific calculator to get to the power, which is a little bit up to 12. And that's going to give us the one point seven nine five, eight six Newtons that these problems all typically are going to have some kind of rounding involved. If you use the table, the table might come up with a slightly different answer than something like Excel, because Excel will not actually round it. Excel we'll use the actual number, which is this number, if you put it into the system with a formula.

This is another way that a test question can also kind of force you to use whatever method they use by using this rounding method, which will result in one method being slightly different than another method in practice. Obviously, the difference is probably in material and doesn't really matter. So then we have the present value is going to be that five, five, six, eight. So in other words, if I was to take this amount here, let's do our division problem. We got the ten thousand divided by, and then we're going to be picking up this divided by one point seven nine five eight six. Now note that's rounded now and that's going to give us the five, five, six, eight and we.

The thirty seven to thirty seven slightly different, it would round to thirty six because I cut off some of those decimals as we did the rounding. If we wanted to figure out the amount that would be in a table, for example, the tables. How do we calculate the tables that we'll use later? You could take this amount and say, let's divide that by ten thousand, and that's going to give us our rate point five, five, six, eight for about once again, there's rounding involved. That's what's going to be basically on the table that will take a look at, although, again, a decimal and rounding may differ slightly. So now let's do this with the Excel type of calculation. So if we have the similar information and we use the Excel format first, using the formula table up top, we would say, OK, I'm going to take the rate, which we would find in whatever.

So it would be in. And that would be the rate of the five percent. Remember that we're using actual years. So I do not need to break that rate down to a monthly rate. But if we were using months, we would have to tie in the rate to the period that we're using. And we would do that if it were a month by dividing by twelve here. The number of periods is then going to be 12. Again, that being in years, the payment is zero because we're not using an annuity. Therefore, we're going to use the present value calculation. And this item, which is not Boldon, is the future value, future value of one being the ten thousand. That gives us our five, five, six, eight. Here are five, five, six eight thirty seven that we had up top.

So that's how we would do it in basically an Excel type of calculation. Now let's use the present value tables, which are going to be down below. And that method, we would simply take the ten thousand and we would multiply it by the proper amount, according to the table, making sure that we're picking up the proper table. Typically there are four. If you're working on a practice problem, present value, two of them, future value, two of them, one for the present value of one, one for the present value of an annuity. This is not an annuity which has one amount, therefore, present value of one, if that's the case. These amounts should be less than one, right? Because it's got to be something smaller than the amount that you're picking up, because it's going to be discounted back to the present value. So we're then going to say that we have ten thousand twelve years, five percent.

So 12 years is way down here. Five percent is right there. So we're going to say that's going to be 12 years at the five percent point five, five, six, eight. So there's the point five, five, six, eight, ten thousand times two point five, five, six, eight is going to give us that five, five, six, eight. Once again, be careful down here. If you're using these tables for something other than a year that you're picking up the proper rate that lines up to the proper periods, meaning, you know, if you're you know, you've got to make the rates in the periods have to line up here. So if you're using something other than years, make sure you're lining those up properly. That rate here, that point five, five, six, eight is similar to what we calculated up top point five, five, six, eight four.

Notice they rounded the rate down to four digits on the table. And so that's going to give you a slightly different number, possibly. And that could be useful again, for test preparers or test questions. You want to force you to use the table and not want you to use a financial calculator or some other method for whatever reason. So now we're going to change it up. Let's say we receive future value. Twenty thousand three years in the future, discount seven percent. Let's do this with the formula again. So we got this formula. We're going to break out into a table type of format, future value now. Twenty thousand.

Then we have the one area to the end, which is going to be one plus the rate seven percent. That, Of course, gives us one hundred and seven percent. We then have the number of periods that it's going to be going into that's going to be this to N, which will be three. If I plug that into the trusty calculator, we would just simply say we have one plus point O seven. That's going to give us one point oh seven. We're going to take that to the power of three. Take it to the power of three. And that's going to give us then this amount down here because we got round in and are going to be involved. Then if we take the twenty thousand twenty thousand divided by the one point two two five oh four, that's going to give us our sixteen three twenty five ninety six about again it's rounded because we had round in that's going to be involved here.

This is actually using the more exact number because we're in Excel. If I take that amount and divide it by twenty thousand, that's going to give us the points eight one eight one six two nine. This is the amount that might be on the table, although again, rounding will be involved and the table will cut it down to, I believe, four digits. And therefore, it's going to be a little less precise, but typically good enough for Decision-Making purposes. So then we have the same information with an Excel type formula. Notice, you can also do the Excel type formula with this little key down below, which is the same thing as the box we used up top, which would be the rate. So three would be the rate, and that would be the seven percent, the number of periods and number of.

The Period is going to be three. Once again, make sure that you understand the number of periods as being whatever they should be, years or months typically. And then we have the repayments. We're not making payments because this is not an annuity. We're just using one. So therefore, that amount is going to be zero or you just have two commas. And then we're going to be picking up the last amount, which is going to be the future value. That being the twenty thousand, that formula then will provide us with the same result because the rounding could be involved. And then if we take a look at the same thing, using the tables, we're going to be taking that twenty thousand times the amount on the table. We're going to pick the three periods, three years at seven percent.

So three years, seven percent, three point eight one six three. So there's two points eight one six three. If we multiply that out, we get the 60 three. Twenty six. That's about the same as this number. Little different, though, because of rounding. You saw the tables only went out four digits. When we calculate the table this way, what that should be on the table, this is what we calculated it to be, what was on the table. But it was rounded to basically four digits point eight one six two. And they rounded it two point eight one six three here from the table. Let's do it again. We got the future value of the thirty thousand years, nine years discount to 12 percent. Let's do it with a formula.

We're going to say, all right, that means thirty thousand is the future value. Now we're going to do the one plus hour to the end one plus our 12 percent to that's one hundred and twelve percent to nine being the number of periods. But not in the trusty calculator. We get one point, one two gives us one hundred and twelve percent. And then we're going to take that to nine. And that's going to give us our two. Our two points are seven seven three, and then they rounded it round here, so it's rounded here, it's more specific in the calculator. I'm going to then remove this. I'm going to say the thirty thousand divided by the two points seven seven three oh eight is going to give us that ten thousand eight one eight.

About 30. And then if I take that amount and I divide it by thirty thousand, that's going to give us the amount that we expect to be on the table. What rounded to four digits, that being the three six oh six. So let's go ahead and check that out. So that means the thirty thousand if we discounted it at the 12 percent for the number of years, nine years. That would give us what we would think of the current value of the ten thousand eight one eight point three zero. If we do that same calculation for Excel, we would say, OK, the rate here is going to be the 12 percent and then the number of periods remembering that we have them in years here. So if they were months, we'd have to make sure to put them in the proper period. That's going to be the nine periods. The payment is going to be zero.

So at this time, we'd represented that with just two to commas. Instead of putting a zero, which is fine as well. Either way, it works. And then we have the future value, which is going to be the one that would be the thirty thousand that Ben would give us the same result going down to the tables. We had the same thing on the tables. So now we're going to take the table amount. We need 12 percent in nine years, 12 percent. And the nine years, the point three, six, three point three, six, three times the thirty thousand gives us that ten thousand eight one eight.

And that ten thousand eight one eight is about the same as this ten thousand eight one eight point three different five point three, Of course, because as we could see, the rates are slightly different, the table rounding to four digits. So we have calculated what we thought should be on the table.

Point three, six, three, one. And it has zero point three six oh six Holon six point six point three six oh six one point three six oh six one. Got things backwards there. I do that less so than you used to, but still do it in any case. There we have it. Multiple different methods.

Future Value Compounded Annually vs Semi Annually

Corporate finance practice problem using one note, we're going to do a future value calculation at this time doing a comparison of compounding annually versus semi-annual, we don't leave generating profits solely to chance. Instead, use corporate finance. Here we are in our practice problem in one note, if you would like to follow along. You're not required to. But if you have access to one note and would like to, we're going to be in the item up top. I'm going to open up this item up top or in the practice problems chapter. We're down here in the 915. That's the 915 future value compounded annually versus Samite annually. I'm going to close this icon up, up to the left so that we then have room to work. We're going to have our information up top.

We're going to be working on multiple different practice problems. The first one is one that we've seen before or similar type of problem. So I'll go through it a little bit more quickly. And then the last bit will be the new item where we're going to be comparing it to semiannual. And that will be the new thing as we go. So if you want to jump forward to the new thing, then you can go to the end. We're going to start and go through the normal kind of process we've seen in the past related to the future value. We're going to have our information up top. We will calculate this in three different ways. One, with the use of the formula to with Excel, three with the tables.

So we've got to invest. Fifteen thousand years, 11 years. The percent is going to be 10 percent. So we're imagining we're investing now. Fifteen thousand now. What is it going to be in terms of future value terms after the period of 11 years this time? We are compounded annually, like we have seen in the past, using the 10 percent item. Once again, Of course, the 10 percent is something that we would have to determine what that rate should be. And that's going to be some part of the estimate. We don't know what the rate should be because, you know, we're estimating into the future as best we can.

So formula wise, it's going to be the future value equals the present value times one plus hour to the end. And we're going to break that formula down into a table type of format, as we've seen in the past. Really think this is good practice to do. Oftentimes I can't help putting together tables, so I recommend doing this in Excel. We do have this problem in Excel as well. So we'll take the present value, that being, Of course, fifteen thousand. Then we're going to be taking this pitch, which is going to be the one plus R to the N one, plus R to the N. It's going to be one. And then the rates are going to be the 10 percent that's going to give us one hundred and ten percent.

Taking that to the end, which is the number of periods that's been in years in our case, which will be 11. That's one of the things we need to keep in mind. If it differentiates, if we're combined in, say, CIMMYT annually or something like that. So let's go ahead and then do the calculation. We got one. Then we're going to add the ten percent point one. That's, Of course, one hundred and ten percent, one point one. And then we're going to take that to the power of that's going to be the little carrot up top, 11, 11 periods, 11 years. That gives us our if I move the decimal place over to eight five three one about noticed this number is rounded here.

And then if I take the trusty calculator here and we multiply that out, taken this time, the 15 15000 that's going to give us our forty two seven ninety six seventy five notes. Again it's rounded. So there we have that calculation for the future value. That's what we would expect in the future value after the 11 years compounded annually, 10 percent rate. Let's think of it in terms of calculating it in a year by year type of calculation. This is really useful if you have Excel, it's easy to do in Excel. I recommend using Excel to do it because it's good practice. So if we then have and it also gives you a better idea of, Of course, what is happening here.

And so we got fifteen thousand where we started and period one, which is year one. And then if we add 15000 to it, which Of course would simply be the fifteen thousand is pulling out the trusty calculator, the 15000 times the ten percent point one for a year. So a year's worth of interest would be that one thousand five hundred. Adding that then to the prior period amounts fifteen thousand. That gives us the sixteen five. If we then go on down and we do the same process on down, taking that sixteen five times the point one that's going to give us the one six five zero. If I add that then to the prior balance of the sixteen five we're going to get then the 18, 150 and so on and so forth. If you do this calculation in Excel, once again, it's easy to do. You can see exactly, you know, what is happening with the compound.

And you could see the interest going up as we go as we compound per period in this case on an annual basis. So there's that calculation. We can see it in a similar format here. This would be more of an Excel type of exercise to kind of calculate it or format your table in a little bit different format of a way. So then we're going to go back down. And now we have Excel. If we did the same calculation in Excel, we can use our little formula count. Elation here, which would basically be that we're going to be taking the I believe it starts with the rate and the rate, and then we're going to say karma, and then we're going to be picking up the number of periods which I believe is 11 here and then zero. That's because it's not an annuity. And then we're going to have the present value, which is fifteen thousand.

I believe that's how that's going to pull forward. We will work this in Excel. Highly recommend putting this into Excel. That would, Of course, give us a quick calculation. Forty two seven ninety six seventy five, which is what we got up here as well. But note that it doesn't give you really, you know, the detail that it would if you saw kind of like the compound in that you can do a running balance with Excel. But that's going to be the most common type of calculation you'll probably see in practice. People will just magically put it into a formula in Excel or a financial calculator. Then the answer appears, and most people don't really understand anything more than that. Right.

So but if you then have the tables, you've got fifteen thousand, then we pick up the amount from the tables, which is going to be the percent and the number of years. So here's the percentage number of periods. We have to make sure to line up the periods and the percentages that are going to be proper. This has been years and rates. So that's going to be the two point five eight oh four. So that's going to be the two point eight five. Let's do that again. This was 10 percent and 11 years, 10 percent, 11 years. Two point eight five three one two point eight five three one. Once again, give us forty two seven sixty nine seven ninety six fifty. It's forty two seven ninety six fifty. So another method to get to the similar calculation. Let's do it again.

This time we're going to do another one in a few years. We're not doing CIMMYT annually yet. Another one in years. Fifteen thousand nineteen years percent, 10 percent. Let's put in this calculation. Future value equals present value, times one plus hour to the end. Doing that with a formula. Fifteen thousand. That's going to be the amount that we invest. Then we're going to take the one plus the rate, 10 percent gives us 110 percent to the power of NPS, which is 19. This time that's going to give us six eleven fifty nine. If we take that amount and multiply it times the fifteen thousand present value, we get ninety one seven thirty eight, sixty four.

If we saw that with the use of of a period by period type of calculation, looking something like this once again using years period zero Rapti 15000, 15000 times ten percent would be one thousand five hundred plus the fifteen thousand brings us to sixteen thousand five, sixteen thousand five times ten percent would be one thousand six fifty one thousand six fifty plus the sixteen five gives us the eighteen one fifty eighteen one fifty then times the ten percent gives us the one eight one five one eight one five plus the 18 150 gives us the 99 sixty five ninety nine sixty five times ten percent gives us the one nine nine six point five one nine nine six point five plus to ninety nine sixty five gives us the twenty one nine, 60, 150 and so on and so forth, bringing us down to the total at the bottom which would be the seventy six seven thirty eight sixty four for the total interest and the total balance.

Ninety one seven thirty eight sixty four. So we got the ninety one seven thirty eight, sixty four that we have here. Similar way to do the calculation. This looks like a very long, tedious way and it would be Of course by hand, but with Excel. Very easy to do. This calculation gives you a much better understanding of how the interest is accumulating when you see it in that format. We could then again do it in Excel, which means we would be taking this formula formula in Excel. I won't break it out again with the Excel formula we've seen a few times this time, but that would give us the balance in a much quicker way as well.

Same way with a financial calculator. If we do this in the tables, then we would take the nineteen periods because it's nineteen years, the period being in years and ten percent. So we take the nineteen down here and the ten percent, which is going to be the six point one one five nine. So six point one one five nine gives us two ninety one seven thirty eight fifty once again tying that out that's going to be the ninety one seven thirty eight sixty four, ninety one seven thirty eight fifty. A little bit different due to rounding. Same scenario we have seen in the past there. Let's do this again. We're going to do it again. This is not counting. Still one more time on the present value in years. So we're going to say the calculation here, this is going to be fifteen years. This is going to be fifteen thousand in eighteen years.

Ten percent. So fifteen thousand present value. Then we're going to take one plus the rate. Ten percent. One hundred and ten percent. That's going to give us the power of. Eighteen. Which is going to give us the five five five point nine nine. If I take fifteen thousand times that amount, we're going to get eighty three, three, ninety eight, seventy six. So then we can do this with the calculation year by year here. Fifteen thousand times, once again, the 10 percent, one thousand five hundred gives us the sixteen five, six, five times 10 percent, one six five zero one six five zero plus two six five gives us the 18, 150 and so on and so forth.

Doing that on out till we get to the eighteen years gives us an ending balance of the eighty three three ninety eight seventy six that means matching the eighty three three ninety eight seventy six. We have the formula calculation over here. If we do that then with a formula similar to the formula rate, which would be this case, the 10 percent number of periods which is going to be eighteen because we're doing this in years payment zero or two, two commas, present value fifteen thousand. Same calculation down here. Then we're going to do the tables on the table side of things which will then take eighteen periods because we're in years and 10 percent per year.

So we're going to take our good old eighteen periods down here and the ten, which is going to be the five point five five nine nine five point five five nine nine that then multiplying that out gives us the eighty three three ninety eight fifty going back up. That's going to give us the eighty three three ninety eight seventy six. There is rounding for the tables. They are rounded to four decimal places, therefore not quite as exact good for practice, but slightly different. So then we have down here now we're going to do the new thing. We have compounded Semi annually. So what is that going to do to our system? We are going to invest fifteen thousand nine years and then 10 percent. But this time it's compounded by the Semi annually. So we have the present value or the future value calculation, present value times one plus or to the end.

But now we get a little bit of an altercation, because when we're thinking about the periods here, we're thinking about semiannual as opposed to annual. So we get the present value. Fifteen thousand and we got our one plus rate to the end. So we're going to take our five percent. Why five percent? Because we need to match the percentage amount up to the periods that will be covered. And now the periods are no longer in years, not nine years, but it's going to be 18 periods, nine times, two periods, and the rate is often given per year. And we have to match the rate to the period. So the rate is given per year, because if you are mad, if you break the rate down to a per month rate, you're going to get to a very small rate. If you deal with yearly rates, then you have the rates that make that are easier to report. It's hard to deal with if you're going to give a rate for a daily rate to be zero point zero zero one, something like that.

So those are harder numbers to just talk about. So we typically deal with rates in the standard format of years and then have to match them from there to what's going to line up to the period. In this case, Simbi, annually, 10 percent, then divided by two to get to the semi annually, and that's going to be the five percent. And so if we take the one plus the one 05 and then we take it to the power of 18, once again, 18 being different here, we're not taking nine because nine is the number of years, but it's compounded Semi annually. Therefore, we have 18 periods that we're going to be considering. And the waiting periods line up not to the annual interest rate, but rather to the interest rate for the periods being covered.

Semiannual is six month interest rates. If it was something other than semiannual, then you could break it out by basically dividing by 12 rate. It would be a monthly rate or something like that. If it's quarterly, you divide by 12 and then multiply times three because there's going to be or divide by 12, and then multiply that times three, because three months in a quarter, you can divide by four or something like that in any case. Then the calculation will be the same once we have these two items lined up. So we get the two forty, sixty six and when we take the fifteen thousand times that to forty sixty six and this is in a percentage format that's going to give us the thirty six 099 twenty six or the thirty six oh nine nine twenty nine.

Now it's useful to run these in Excel. So you kind of see the difference of compounding annual and semiannual a little bit easier. You can do that here as well by basically comparing it to what we have done up top. So I'll just go back to the last one we did up top where we have fifteen thousand eighteen years. So we had eighteen periods still here, but this was eighteen years instead of semi-annual for nine years, and the percent, which was 10 percent and we got to the eighty three three ninety eight fifty here. Now if you consider here, we're still talking about half the time period, nine years at 10 percent. But we're compounded on the semi. So you might run some different scenarios to get an idea of what the compounding semi annually would do.

And again, I would recommend doing that in Excel and doing this type of calculation. But you also might want to do the running balanced calculation down here in Excel, because that really gives you a better picture of what's going on from period to period. So let's try to do that running balance. We're going to say, all right, if we start off with the 15000, we're now going to say the period. One is 750. Period, one is 750, because period one is no longer a year. But it's a similar year. It's half a year every half a year. So that means we're going to take this fifteen thousand dollar amount times, not the 10 percent, but times the point five percent, five percent point five or five percent. Get the 750, the 750 plus to 15000. It's going to give us 15, 750.

And then if we take that 15, 750, MS can delete this whole thing. If I take that 15, 750 and I multiply it times point oh five, then we're going to get these seven, eight, seven. If I take that seven, eight, seven and add it to the prior balance of 15, 750, we're going to get these 16, five, 30, 750. If I take that amount and multiply it times the point of five, then we're going to get twenty six, eighty eight and so on and so forth. Same kind of process. But we're going out to 19 periods. These periods, however, are not years rather being Simbi years every six months. And then we get to about thirty six 099. Twenty nine.

So if you compare this kind of amortization table or not, you know, this kind of table to a table that firms for compounding annually or monthly or something like that, then it gives you a better feel of what the different compounding will do. We see the end result here at the thirty six 099 twenty six and the thirty six oh nine nine twenty nine twenty nine twenty nine thirty six oh nine nine twenty nine. OK, so then if we did this with a formula in Excel, we have a little bit of a slight change here as well. We're going to take the rate, which is going to be that 10 percent we can pick up with a formula which would be in this case in Selby three. So it would be in Selby three, the 10 percent. But we have to have that percentage of line up to the number of periods in the periods that are compounding semi-annually.

Therefore, I'm going to take that and divide it by two. So we divide it by two. That's going to give us our five percent. And then comma number of periods, the number of periods now is going to be nine years. But we're going to compound semi annually. Therefore, I'm going to take that nine years, times two, and that'll give us our eighteen. So now we have 18 periods representing every six months, which need to match the percentage, not on a yearly basis, but monthly basis. Therefore, we take the yearly rate divided by two commas, and then we get the payments. There are no payments because this is not an annuity. And then comma and we pick up the amount that was put in present value, the fifteen that once again will give us our same amount.

Thirty six oh nine nine twenty nine thirty six 099. Twenty nine. And then we have the similar situation with the tables you have to be careful with with the periods that we have. So we get the fifteen thousand that we're going to pick the amount up from the table. It's going to be nine years, but we're not looking at nine years because we're looking at periods in which it's going to be compounded semi-annually. Therefore it's going to be 18 periods and then the rate is not 10 percent, but once again, five percent, because the rate needs to be tied to the period that is being covered, which is semi-annual, therefore, five percent. So we're looking five percent at 18, 18 periods at five percent per period. So 18 periods down here and then five percent.

What's going to be the two point four oh, six six point two point four oh six six of fifteen thousand times to two point four 066 gives us the thirty six 099, which is close to what we have over here at thirty six 099. Twenty nine due to the fact that we have once again the rounding on the tables, it pulls out the percent out to four decimal. So that's going to be useful enough for practice. It's going to be a little bit different than what would be there if you used the calculations and didn't round and note that book problems, test questions, might use that to try to force you to use one method versus another. So be careful about that.

Present Value (PV) Decision Making

Corporate finance practice problem within one note. Present value RPV decision making. Scenario being what? We'd rather have less money today or more money, but have it at some point in the future. Get ready. It's time to take your chance with corporate finance. Here we are in one note. If you would like to follow along in one note and have access to it, you're not required to. But if you have access to one note and would like to. We're going to be in the tab on the left hand side, opening this up or in the practice problems chapter. We're down here in the 916, the present value PJV Decision making. I'm going to close this back up. Our general scenarios are going to be what if we get paid today versus getting paid at some point in the future? How much less would I accept today as opposed to having to wait to get paid at some point in time in the future? This is kind of like the classic lottery type of question.

If you win a lottery or something like that and you're trying to figure out what if they give me a lump sum payment today, but it's less than the future value if they give it to me at some point in the future or possibly in some kind of series of payments in the future, same kind of scenario. Those types of scenarios come up quite often, both in business and personal decision making. And then we want to think about how we would make those decisions. Obviously, if we have the ability to get the money today, we would like to have it today, because then we could do stuff with it. We could either spend it and have fun with it or we can invest it and hopefully have it grow. If we have it in the future, then we don't have that opportunity. So here's going to be the first scenario. We'll run a couple of these.

So we're going to say the amount is going to be the amount in 50 years. We get 50 thousand dollars. So what if we get 50 thousand dollars in 50 years or one thousand dollars today and the discount rate is 10 percent? Now, obviously, when you're thinking about this type of decision making process, if you're thinking 50 years, if you need the money right now, then you're probably saying, well, that's a pretty easy choice. I need a thousand dollars in 50 years. I'm not really thinking about 50 years. So, I mean, I'll just take the thousand dollars right now. It may not be a big choice, but if you're in a situation where you possibly don't need the one thousand at this point in time and you're saying, oh, fifty thousand in 50 years, then I might I mean, you know, I might be around and retired at that point in time. Maybe the fifty thousand will be useful at that point.

Seems like a big difference between the two. Possibly it would be worthwhile then to wait it out and get the fifty thousand at the end of the time period. Well, we can use our present value kind of calculation to do this kind of comparison. Same kind of calculation we saw in the past. That being, we'll take the future amount if it's a one lump sum payment. In this case, we're not talking about an annuity, one lump sum payment 50 years from now. If I can pull it back then to today and then do the comparison to what we have today. So that's going to be the idea. In order to do that, though, we need a discount rate, which, Of course, is difficult to come by.

What should the discount rate be? And we have to take multiple things into consideration with the discount rate. And that could be well, if I had the thousand dollars today, I can do stuff with it. I can spend it. And you might think, well, you know, that's not a comparable thing. But obviously, if I can spend it now and use it at this point in time, that is, you know, worthwhile, we can. But it's hard to get a discount rate from that. We could also take the thousand dollars and think about, well, what could I invest it in if I could invest it and have it grow? And if we're saying, I think I can have it grow by like 10 percent or something like that, then maybe that would be a discount rate that we could use.

We could also consider inflation that could be involved in this as well. Inflation might be a factor in our calculation of the. But just note, it's not the only factor. Obviously, the purchasing power of money will go down. But we also need to consider the opportunity cost that's going to happen here. If I had the thousand dollars today, I could do something with it at this point in time, spend it, or if I were to invest it, I can get a return on it. And that would be the opportunity cost. We'd have to take that into consideration when figuring out a discount rate. So then once we have it, if we say we think it's going to be 10 percent, then we can use our present value formula here or multiple methods, the formula, financial calculator, Excel or your tables, then to to figure out this item, bringing it back to the future time period, and then seeing whether or not it be greater or less than the amount that we would receive today.

So we're bringing this fifty thousand back from fifty years in the future back to the present, using the 10 percent discount rate. If we use our formula, we would take the fifty thousand here for the future value. Then we're going to do this part at the bottom one plus hour to the end, just like we've seen in the past. I'll do this quicker because we've seen it in the past. So we're going to say this is one plus the 10 percent, that being the discount rate that we would have to come up with. That's one hundred and ten percent. And then we've got the number of periods taking it to the power of 50, the number of periods that gives us this amount. And then if. We take the fifty thousand and divide it by the one one seven point three nine. We're then going to get the four twenty five ninety three.

Obviously now the four twenty five ninety three is less than one thousand dollars. So you'd think we would want one thousand now. We'd want one thousand today. Obviously, again, if we need the one thousand dollar spending, it would still be worthwhile. While you might say, well, if I spend it, I'm not going to get the fifty thousand in the future. But you're still using it when you need to use it in the present. And if you were, say, to invest it and get a return of something like the 10 percent and whatnot, then you would rather have the one thousand still, because you would think it would be beneficial then to even the fifty thousand in fifty years. So we can also do that calculation and say in Excel if we had an Excel type of calculation. Same kind of thing.

I won't go over the calculation again. But you could use the present value formula to bring back the fifty thousand to the present, and then you can simply compare it to the one thousand dollars here. Also note and we'll do this in Excel. I won't do it here in one note, but you might want to go through the Excel practice problem because it can help you to calculate the break-even point using a goal, which seems like a what if analysis type of calculation fairly easily. So in other words, I can use kind of like the present value function to do a goal, seek a type of calculation within Excel and try to figure out, well, what would the rate be in order for this to be a break, even analysis. In other words, when I was figuring this out, this 10 percent is something that I had to come up with.

I had a guess what that would be in order to come up with a logical type of calculation to come up with the figures here. But I might say, well, what then, you know, what would that rate need to be in order for the two things to be the same? And if we go down, then we can kind of calculate that rate. That would then be our break even rate. And if we consider it that way, then we might say, OK, if that's the consideration, then if I if I consider this discount rate as anything above the 10 percent above I'm sorry, the eight point one, three or so forth, then you would think that we would want to take the one thousand. And if you think about this anywhere below the eight point one, so on, then it might be worthwhile to then wait it out and get the fifty at the end of the time period.

So it's kind of our break even rate. Let's do it. Let's do another kind of item with the table here. Table calculations, as we've seen before. We've got fifty thousand. We want to bring it back. We're talking years in terms of a period of fifty years at the ten percent. So here's the ten percent column, 50 years all the way at the bottom point zero eight five that then if we multiply that out gives us the four twenty five again it's not exact because the tables are rounded. If I was to look at the actual number of the table, you would think it would be point zero eight five one nine, which would give us the four twenty five ninety three, but close enough for our determination factors here when we do this kind of calculation. Let's do another one. We've got the amount.

Ten years. How about a hundred thousand in ten years or an amount of fifty thousand today? So we can get fifty thousand today or we can get one hundred thousand in ten years. Same process. We would have to come up with the discount rate and then we're going to pull this amount in the future back to the present, and then we'll be able to figure this out. This is similar to what you would do with a lottery payment or something like that. But you would have annuities. And we'll talk more about annuities later if you've got multiple payments that are going to happen versus a lump sum payment in the present. But, you know, same kind of idea. We want to take all the future payments, bring them back to a current dollar amount, compare it to what we would get in the current dollar amount.

We would have to once again come up with that discount rate considering possibly inflation and possibly what we can do with the fifty thousand at this point in time. Obviously, if we needed the fifty thousand at this point in time for our current needs, then, you know, we're going to need the fifty thousand. It's worth more to us possibly at this point in time, because we need it. But if we don't really need it at this point in time, and we could invest it or we can do without it and then wait it out for ten years, then what's going to be the discount rate? What can we do with that? Fifty thousand to grow it? In the meantime, what would be the opportunity cost, in other words, if we had fifty thousand.

So we came up with nine percent. We could do this multiple ways. Now we're going to use the present value to bring back the future payment of one hundred thousand back to the present. Compare it to the fifty thousand to see whether it is higher or lower to it. So we're taking that one hundred thousand. And now we're going to basically take the bottom component, one plus R to the N. So one plus the rate of nine percent. One hundred and nine percent to the power of ten. That's going to give us this number. And then if we do the final calculation, one hundred thousand divided by the two points three, six, seven, three, six, we get forty two to forty one. That number is less than fifty thousand. So in that situation, once again, we'd want fifty thousand.

Even if we're not going to spend it at this point in time, possibly because we would think that we can invest it in some way and possibly make a nine percent return on it, and if that's the case, then that's what we would typically want to do. Now, we can also think about this in Excel. So the same kind of idea with Excel, we can use the present value to get to that. Forty two to forty one. I won't do it here. If you want to check out Excel, you can look at that. You can compare that to the fifty thousand, and then you can once again use that goal, seek to try to say, OK, I see that, you know, if it was nine percent, then I would be better off taking the fifty thousand.

But how low does that percent need to go before it's a break, even if it's a wash between the two? And if we do that, a break even type of analysis, and we can use this goal in order to do it in Excel. I recommend just taking a look at that, because it's an easy way. And it's something that just to keep in mind that you can basically do algebra on like a formula with a, you know, a trial and error type of method. And Excel can give you some results. And that makes it a lot easier to use formulas that you kind of know. And then back into an unknown within the equation on it. So it's useful, useful to take a look at.

So I would take a look at it. But in any case, if you come to that seven point one seven, that's when you would think the 50 and the 50 possibly would be the same. And then that means that anything over that seven point one seven, you would think that you would make the money today. And anything below that you might want it in, in the future. And then if we go to another one, we can also use the tables. Of course, if we use the tables, I said 10 years and nine percent, 10 years and nine percent. So there's the nine percent. Here's the 10 years. The point for two to four. So there's two point four, two to four. So the one hundred thousand times two point four, two, two, four gives us two four two two four zero.

And that once again, below the fifty thousand same calculation. It's slightly different from what we had up here because the tables are rounded to four decimals. If we took it out exactly. It would be four point four, two, two, four, one, one. And we get a more exact number. But the tables are good enough for us for both Decision-Making purposes, Of course. And then if we go back down, let's do this again. Now we're going to say, I can get this little box. You don't need that. We got ten years. How about one hundred and ten thousand or fifty thousand today? So we can get one hundred and ten thousand in ten years or fifty thousand today. And now we're going to say we think the discount rate is only five percent. We think we can only get the five percent discount rate.

Consider an opportunity, cost inflation and whatnot. So we can then, OK, let's bring that one hundred and ten thousand back to today's units. So we got the one hundred and ten and then we've got the one plus the five percent. One hundred and five percent to the power of ten. One point six to eight, nine. One hundred and ten thousand divided by that. One point six to eight eight nine is sixty seven five, thirty point four six. So now this amount that we would bring back is greater than the fifty thousand because in part of the lower discount rate. So in that situation, if we think we're only going to have a discount rate of the five percent in one hundred and ten thousand and ten years, you would think that we would want then if all else being equal, if we didn't need to spend the fifty thousand today to get the one hundred and ten and the fifty years could be a good investment.

So we can also think about that and say, all right, well, what would be the break even point if I do the same calculation in Excel using the present value formula, I can come up to the same number here, compare it to the fifty thousand. And then again, we can make the break even point and think about the break even point, because we would clearly then be asking, well, I don't know about this discount rate. Five percent is kind of low. Maybe I can take that money and earn a greater return on it than the five percent. So what? Know how high of a return before this would be a break even type of analysis. And we're talking eight point two. Oh three.

So therefore, if I was to consider that discount rate at something greater than eight points to oh three, then we might want the money, the fifty thousand today. If it was less than eight point two oh three, we would come up to the conclusion that we had before, which we might then want to wait it out for ten years and pick up what we have there. And then we have the present value table. Same kind of analysis we're going to say now. We've got ten years at five percent, though. So here's the ten years and here's our I'm sorry, the five percent and here's the ten years. The point six one three nine. So there's the point six one three nine. So one hundred and ten times two point six one three nine once again, getting to that sixty seven, five, twenty nine, which is less than fifty.

Therefore we would take the fifty this amount, not exactly the same as what we got and the other methods because the tables are rounded to four digits. If we were to see the table and more than four digits, it might be something like point six, one three nine one three and so on to give us a more exact number of sixty, seventy five, thirty, forty six as opposed to the sixty seven five twenty nine even. But for most Decision-Making purposes, that's well within the range for materiality, for a good decision.

Present value Different Discount Rates Side by Side

Corporate finance practice problems using one note, present value, different discount rates, we're going to do that with a side by side comparison. Don't leave profits solely to chance. Instead, use corporate finance. Here we are in one note. If you have access to one note and would like to follow along, you're not required to. But if you would like to, where in this tab on the left hand side, we're in the practice problems. And then down in the nine one nine present value, different discount rates side by side chapter. Closing this out with the icon on the left hand side. Also note, if you have access to one note, you might want to check out this immersive reader, which will actually go through text files and go through it and give you translation options to other languages and even read it through in terms of English or other languages with the translation may not be as useful for this practice problem.

But we do have chapters that we add to this resource from time to time. And you can use that to basically translate if you would like to, and even here, the information in the translation format. So we're going to have our information up top on the left hand side. We're going to go through the calculation in a few different ways in the blue areas down below. This will be a present value calculation. We're going to be comparing side by side the difference of interest rates. We'll do the calculation a few different ways, one, with the mathematical formula to with an Excel type of calculation, which would be similar to a financial calculator type of calculation.

And then we'll take a look at it with tables as well, often use and book problems, information. We're going to say in 30 years, we will have an amount of one hundred thousand. So we're imagining a situation where we're going to get one hundred thousand and thirty years. What would it be in terms of today's dollars? Well, to do that, we would have to get some kind of discount rate. The discount rate typically takes into consideration time value of money, possibly inflation. In other words, what could we do with that money if we had it now and then? Think about basically reversing that out, right. If I had the money today, I can do something with it or invest it. So I want to take into consideration the time value of money.

And you have to take into consideration those factors basically to figure a discount rate, which could be appropriate. This is a guess. And we could use multiple rates. You could start to experiment with the rates that would be used, which we'll start with here. And we're saying, well, what if it was 12 percent? What if it was five percent? We'll do a side by side comparison. We'll start it out with this formula. The mathematical formula today, and we'll compare it to money today of the twenty thousand. So you can imagine a situation, possibly a price situation, you winning something or something like that. And they say we'll give you one hundred thousand and thirty years or we'll give you twenty thousand today, that type of scenario. And obviously, if you need the money today, then it wouldn't be too difficult of a question that I need it now.

But if you don't need it right now, then you might say, hey, you know, maybe I'll wait 30 years if it's going to be a significantly more amount. So that's going to be the scenario. So we're going to bring this one hundred thousand back to the present day. The twenty thousand is already in the present day. You don't need to do anything for that. We need to compare it from the same thing to the same thing. Apples to apples, as they say, by bringing the one hundred thousand back to the present. We'll do that first. Mathematically present value equals the future value times one over one plus hour to the end.

The future value being in this case, the one hundred thousand we will receive in the future are then being the rate, which will be the differential factor of 12 percent or five percent in the number of periods that being 30 in this case, periods being years. So if we break this calculation, I'm going to break it down into a table type of format, a useful tool to use. We basically want the numerator and the denominator and the far right column and then any other kind of calculations I need, like this bottom calculation, I'll pull into the inner column. So, for example, for A and B scenarios, we have one hundred thousand one hundred thousand. That's going to be the future value. Same for each. Then we've got the one plus R to the N. That's going to be the denominator here. The bottom part, which I'm going to pull into the inner column here and here and do our calculations there.

So one that's going to be this one plus the rate, that's the differential factor, which is going to be either twelve or five percent. And that if we add those up, we get the one hundred and twelve percent or one hundred and five percent. Note when you're doing these calculations, you ought to be thinking about my record in this in terms of decimals or percents as you enter this into a calculator. And then we're going to say we need to take that to the thirty periods, to the end, to the thirty periods. So that's going to be, you know, thirty. So once again, remember that if you're using a financial calculator or some type of calculator, you need to take it to the power of thirty. So that's one hundred and twelve one oh five to the power of thirty, which is going to give us the.

Twenty nine point nine five nine nine two noting that this is going to be rounded out to this decimal, rounded out to this decimal over here. Note that if you're using some kind of test question, they may actually force you to round it out to so many decimals, like three decimals to decimals for decimals. And they might use that to see if you're following the directions or using some particular format of calculation. So be careful with instructions and things like test questions probably wouldn't matter in practice because those rounding deviations would not be material enough most likely to change the decision making process, but can't be utilized and test questions.

And then the present value, if we take the final calculation, is the future value of the hundred thousand here divided by the denominator which we came to here. That's going to be the three, three, three, seven point seven nine and the twenty three one thirty seven seventy four that we have on this comparison. So we could see the differences between the twelve and the five percent if we compare either of those to the twenty thousand, if we got today, if we consider our discount rate, if we're estimating the discount rate to be 12 percent, then this one would come out below. Right. We wouldn't want option A, but if we consider the discount rate to be only five percent, then we might say that this twenty three thousand comes out higher. So we may then choose one hundred thousand in thirty years.

We may still not choose it. We might say, hey, I need the money now, so I'd rather have it now. But if we could hold on to the money and we're saying, hey, you know, the hundred is going to be worth more based on the discount rate that we used. And I don't need it right now. You know, I'm going to let the money, you know, grow at that point. Then possibly we might choose option B, if we were to figure out the factor in a table, this is going to be this number divided by one hundred thousand. And this is how you can think about how they come up with the factoring tables, which will take a look at later tables often used for practice problems. Let's do it again. We can do the same type of calculation this time.

We're going to just consider if we used a financial calculator or say, Excel type a calculator. And we've basically seen this in prior chapters. So I won't do the calculation for both of these and say what would happen in Excel. We do have this problem in Excel. So you can take a look at it in Excel and run the calculation. But we could see these two. We could see the same two for A and B, the net result. Also note that if you're using Excel, the next question you might have, if you're comparing these two and you're saying, OK, well, what would be the interest rate, which would be the break even kind of interest rate, meaning when would these two options be the same? When would it be this discount rate taking the present value of one hundred thousand to equal the present day dollar amount of twenty thousand, which could be a fair question to ask.

It might help you with your determination process. So instead of just randomly picking interest rates here that you think might be applicable, then why don't we determine the interest rate, which would make these two options, even basically the break even point. Now, in Excel, they have a system that you can use called goal. So once again, I recommend using Excel, taking a look at the practice problem in Excel, and we'll use that tool of Gauci to kind of figure out the rate, which in this case would be the five point five one one three, which would basically be that break even rate. So we'll continue on here. The next one is the tables so we can use the same kind of thing with the calculation of the tables. One hundred thousand one hundred thousand. Then we want to look at the tables for the twelve percent, thirty years and five percent thirty years.

So if we look at this, we're going to say, alright, table, make sure you're picking up the correct table. Present value of one, not an annuity, 12 percent here at thirty years. Thirty years is way down here. Twelve percent thirty years point three, three point oh three, three, four. So that's where this zero point zero three three four is coming from here. And that once again gives us to that three, three, four. And then we've got the one hundred thousand at the five percent. So thirty years. Five percent. Five percent. Thirty years would be down here. Point one, seven four one.

So hold on to say five percent. Thirty years at five percent. So five percent, 30 years is point two, three, one, four point two, three, one, four, and if we multiply these out one hundred thousand times point oh three, three, four, three, three, four zero, 100000 times zero point two, three, four, one four. Is that twenty three, one, four, two. Notice that these two amounts may be slightly different than these two amounts to three one thirty seven, seventy four, for example, and 30. And so this one for example, is twenty three. One thirty seven. Seventy four versus. Twenty three, one forty.

And that's because we've rounded the tables or the tables have been rounded to four digits, which are not quite as exact meaning if I go back up top, these are actually a decimals a little bit further out point oh, three, three, three, seven, eight, and point two, three, one, three, seven, seven, if we take it out further than four digits here. Point zero three three, four and point two, three, one, four. The tables are typically fine for normal decision making purposes. But once again, if using test questions, they can use that difference in order to restrict multiple choice answers and try to force you to use something like the tables, possibly trying to get the financial calculator either out of your hands or make it obsolete by making the answer key. More specific. Taking into consideration rounded.

Present Value Planning Scenario

Corporate finance practice problem in one note. Present value with planning scenarios, scenarios that will include calculations for the present value of annuities, as well as present value of one, don't leave profits solely to chance. Instead, use corporate finance. Here we are in one note. If you have access to one note and would like to follow along, you're not required to. But if you have access and would like to turn the tab up top here or in the practice problems, we're down here in the 920 present value planning scenario chapter. Also note that if you have access to one note, you might want to use the tool of the immersive RETER that gives the option of actually hearing the text when there's text files within it. It can also convert to Spanish, and you can also then listen to it in Spanish, although it's going to have the translations from text to Spanish.

So it's a couple of translations, but might be useful. We have that information oftentimes with the chapters that would be down here related to these chapters. So if you have down here for the text, for the practice problems right there. And the same one for the 920. You might be able to get and then be able to translate it and possibly hear it in multiple languages. All right. Closing this back out. We're going have our information up top. We'll go through that information in the blue area down below. Here's going to be our scenario to start with. How much must you invest to get fifteen thousand in the future nine years from now? So our question is the lump sum that we're going to put in at this point in time. If it were to grow, then how much would we have to put in now at this one point in order to, in nine years, get fifteen thousand? We'll do this.

This is a present value of one type of calculation. We'll do a similar type of calculation with an annuity. Meaning how much might we have to invest each year to build up to a certain amount? And that'll be in the second half of our practice problem here. First off, just note, this could be a little bit confusing to just think about the fact that this is a present value type of calculation, because we're thinking about how much we'd have to put in now to get to some point in the future. And you might start thinking, well, maybe I should do that by basically just picking amounts that I would put in right now and then do a future value calculation, which you could do. But that would be a trial and error type of scenario.

It would be faster to say, OK, if my goal is to get to fifteen thousand in nine years, then I want to take that fifteen thousand and present it to bring it back to the current period. And that's how much I would have to put in today in one lump sum for it to grow to the future value. So those two calculations are related, Of course, present value and future value. So that's how we'll be pulling this back then. That's nine years out into the future. So that's going to be our period. And then the rate is what we would have to decide. We have to say, well, what rate do we think it will be? We have to pick that out using inflation and possibly using what the alternative for money would be, which would be the opportunity cost of money.

What else could we do with it if we had it today? How much could we get in terms of gains on it or investments in it? So we have our formula down below. We're going to break this formula out. Present value equals future value times one over one. Plus, I'm going to break that out into a table type of format. Here we have this in Excel two, if you want to check it out in Excel. You can look at it there as well. Future value. We're going to pull that out to the outside. So this is where we expect to be. That's going to be the future value, basically, the numerator. And then we're going to have one plus R to the N, so one plus R to the N and do the calculation. There's one.

The R is going to be the 12 percent, one plus 12 percent. It's one hundred and twelve percent. Note that if you're putting this into a calculator, be careful that you're dealing with rounding and you're dealing with percentages. So make sure. Are you looking at in terms of a percent, which would be point one, one, two, or I'm sorry, which would be 112 percent or a decimal, which would be the one point one to on the decimal. We're taking that then to the end. That's going to be the number of periods in our case where our periods are years and we have nine of them. So we're going to take that to N. So that's going to be the one hundred and twelve percent to the power of nine carat nine.

So we're going to take that out and that's going to give us about if we round it, two point seven seven three zero eight. Remember, there is rounding that's going to be involved in these and you have to take those into consideration. If you're doing test questions, make sure that you're following the directions as to how far out they ask you to round. Then the present value is going to be this. Fifteen thousand divided by the two point seven seven three oh eight that's going to give us the five four oh nine 15. So five four oh nine 15. Then that means that we would take the five four oh nine 15 is how much we would have to invest today if we had the rate at 12 percent and then nine years to get to that fifteen thousand.

So that's going to be the first way we can calculate it. If we take this amount, that's five four oh nine fifteen, divided by fifteen thousand. That's how we can basically construct the tables and we'll do the same calculation in terms of the tables shortly. So down here we have Excel. If you do this in Excel, you could populate this in Excel. We will work through this in Excel with our present value calculation, similar to a financial calculator type of situation where you would take the rate, which would be the 12 percent. And then the second sale that we would pick up is the number of periods in this case, nine. Note that we're talking about years here.

We're not talking about months. And therefore, just make sure you're got the correct period there. And then we're not putting anything in for the payments here because the payments are used for an annuity. And this is the present value of one. And then the future value is going to be the fifteen thousand that once again would give us that answer of five thousand for 09 15, much easier. Then we're going to go down and take a look at the tables often used for book problems. Make sure you're picking up the correct table. This is not an annuity, but the present value of one. Therefore, these numbers, you would expect them to be less than one in the table because really you're taking some number in the future, bringing it back.

So you would multiply it by something less than one. If it was an annuity table, you would consider or believe or think that you would be multiplying it times something more than one. Considering the fact that you're taking that payment, which will be reoccurring over time. So we're going to do the table time here at 12 percent. Nine years or nine periods. So there's. Is that right? 12 percent. Nine periods, 12 percent. Nine periods is going to be down here, 12 and nine point three, six oh six. So there's two point three six oh six multiplying the 15000 times a point three six oh six gives us that five four oh nine. Slightly different from what we got here, because the tables are rounded to four digits. Remember that we calculated it at point three six oh six one zero and so on. And it is rounded down here.

Be careful of the rounding with test questions. Let's take a look at another one. This is going to be a present value of one. Then we'll get to the annuities. We'll do this one a little bit more quickly. So we're going to say, what if I want to get to twenty thousand in seventeen years and we have a rate that we're assuming to be seven percent. So once again, we're going to basically take that twenty thousand we're going to be at in twenty years and then bring it back to the current period. That then would be the lump sum that we would have to put in today for it to grow at that rate, to get to twenty thousand in seventeen years. You can also think about this and say, what if I just start using the future value calculation and I just start guessing numbers and see how close it'll get to the 20000? You could do that.

And you could use a goal six in Excel to do that as well. But it would be faster if you want to get an exact number to do it in the reverse format. Take your objective. Twenty thousand in the future. Bring it back. Present value to the current point. That's how much you would have to put in in a lump sum to get there. Once again, future value times or over one plus or to the in future value is going to be twenty thousand. That's our goal. The rate seven percent, the number of periods. Seventeen in years, not months. So we're going to say the future value is going to be that twenty thousand that's going to be on the outside that I'm going to be put in.

And then internally we're going to take the one plus R to the M. That's this calculation one plus R to the N, basically making it like a tax type of format, you know, a table format of this algebraic calculation. And then the one plus seven percent. Be careful that you're talking about percentages and decimals here. So one, you can represent as one hundred percent, right. Plus seven percent would be one hundred and seven percent or one plus seven percent would be zero point zero. Seven plus one would be one point oh seven. And then if we then take that to the power of the number of periods, that's n which is seventeen, that would then give us this amount rounded. So we're taking the one or seven percent to the power of or a carrot of seventeen giving. That's approximately this number. Be careful of rounding.

And then the present value would then be the twenty thousand divided by that. And that's going to give us the three of the six three three one point four nine. So that would mean that if we put a lump sum in today, six, three three, one point four nine at the seventeen percent, after 17 years, we'd hit our goal hopefully. That's our calculation of twenty thousand. You could test that out by looking at the future value calculation. If you so choose, then we're going to go down and take a look at that in an Excel calculation. We do this in Excel, if you want to take a look at that. And it would be a nice quicker calculation, present value calculation, same present value calculation used for both an annuity and present value of one, although slightly different components.

What will be different? The rate is going to be pulled in the rate. Then they got the number of the periods. The number of periods would be seventeen in years here. This is where the difference would be the payment. We're not talking payments because that's an annuity term. That's why it's going to be zero. Instead, we use the future value of twenty thousand. That would give us that same number. Let's take a look at it in terms of the table table time. Same thing. Table time now. Seventeen and seven percent. So seven percent, 17 years. So there's seven percent. Seventeen years would be down here at the point three one six six.

So there's two point three one six six twenty thousand times two point three one six six gives us these six three, three, two, slightly different than the same calculation we did up here because the tables are rounded to four digits. If we were to take the table out of more than four digits, we could see that we came to the point three one six five seven by taking this amount divided by twenty thousand. That's how you can construct the table. Point three one six five seven is rounded down here. Two point three one six six. Let's take a look at an annuity type of scenario now. So how much would you invest to get each period? Eight thousand for 15 years at 11 percent. So now we're saying I would like to put in a lump sum at this point in time and get paid a fixed amount, a thousand per.

Yea, for some period of time, 15 years. So how much would we have to put in today to basically do that? So what we want to do then is present the value of the annuity payments here. So now we've got a number of payments. We want a present value of the annuity, bringing this series of payments back into simply the current day. And that's going to be how we basically come to that calculation. So let's take a look at that. We'll do that a couple of different ways, once again with a formula up top, and then we'll take a look at it in terms of tables as well. So we'll do this in terms of a formula. It'll be a little bit more complex. I'm going to put the C on the outer column here. So that's going to be basically the payment that's going to be on the outer column.

And then we're going to have the numerator and denominator that's we're going to pull into the inner column and then we'll have an inner column for some of this business up top on the numerator where we have a lot more detail going on. So we're going to break this algebra out step by step into basically a table type of format. So we've got the eight thousand that's going to be the amount of the payments, the amount that we're going to receive or that we want each period, which is each year. Then I'm going to look at the numerator, which is going to be one minus all the stuff. I'm going to start with one up top. Then on the inside, we're going to pull in the one plus R to the negative end. That's what we're going to figure here, one plus R to the negative.

And we get the answer to that. And then we'll take one minus that answer. So it's going to be one plus the rate, 11 percent. Remember, be careful with the percentages and decimals. So 100 percent plus 11 percent or R one plus zero point one one gives you one hundred and eleven percent. And then we're going to take that to the number of periods, to the number of periods, negative number of periods, which is 15. So one hundred and eleven percent to fifteen fifteen is going to give us about twenty point nine zero. So take into consideration rounding here as you're thinking about these calculations. And notice, this is being worked on in Excel. So we're actually using the actual numbers when we do these calculations.

Even though, you know, we're taking it out to how many decimal places are here, but Excel will have the actual numbers. So be careful with the rounding. So then we're going to be taking the one minus that amounts to one minus this amount that's going to give us about seventy nine points, one zero percent. And then we have the numerator. Now, that's the entire numerator. We're going to divide that by the denominator, which is once again the rate, and that's going to be the 11 percent. So the seventy nine point one divided by 11 is about then this seven point one nine. Be careful in how you represent these percent or Norn percent items here. And then we're going to take that and multiply it times the eight thousand.

That's going to give us our fifty seven five twenty six ninety six. So there's our fifty seven. And notice this rate here is actually this. If we pulled it out to more decimals and this is what you would expect to see on a table. So that means if we had the fifty seven fire, twenty six ninety six, then you would think that that would be equivalent to the annuity for the eight thousand for fifteen years, and that would be hopefully enough to then at the eleven percent receive then the eight thousand for the 15 year period. So that's a fairly long calculation. We can also see that calculation down here with if you used Excel or financial calculator much more quickly in Excel, it would be looking at something like this. We'd use the same PV type of calculation, present value calculation.

We would take the rate, which would be then that 11 percent comma the number of periods fifteen once again, then comma. Now we're going to be using the payments because this is going to be an annuity calculation and we're talking a payment each time. That's going to be eight thousand. And then we don't need the future value of not using it at this time. That's why we can use the same present value for an annuity or present value of one with that distinction, that difference. There's fifty seven five twenty six ninety six again. Then we can also do this with the use of the tables, making sure that we're picking up the proper table this time the annuity table, as opposed to the present value of once we have our eight thousand. Now we would expect this number down here not to be less than one, but greater than one from the table.

And we're looking for fifteen and 11 percent. Let's go to the table time, table time, annuity time, 11 percent, 15 periods. That's going to be the seven point one nine oh nine. So there's the seven point one nine oh nine times the eight thousand. There is once again the fifty seven five twenty seven twenty that fifty seven five twenty seven twenty maybe slightly different than the fifty seven five twenty six ninety six because of rounding on the table to four digits. Note that we calculated up top that it would be about seven point one nine zero eight seven eight, which they then rounded to one point one nine oh nine. Let's do it one more time. Another problem for an annuity type of calculation, how much must you invest to get each period? The amount of sixty thousand for thirty five. Years, if we assume the rate to be 10 percent.

So now we're going to say, OK, how much would I have to put in today in order for thirty five years to get 60 thousand? And then we're using the rate, the discount rate of the 10 percent. We're going to do that with a formula. Once again, this is an annuity type of calculation, basically present value in the annuity, this series of payments, which will give us the lump sum that we would have to put in today in order to receive that basically annuity kind of calculation. So we got C times the one minus one plus IRR interest to the negative end divided by I. I'm going to put these two items on the outer column of our table. We're basically making a tax return type of format here that will break this algebraic problem into.

So we've got C in the outer column, and then we're going to pull into the inner column, this one minus this top portion. We're going to break out the numerator into some more nuance, nuance of the numerator. So we're going to say one and then minus the one plus I to the negative in which is this portion one plus I to the negative in. There's the one, there's the rate 10 percent. Be careful of the decimals and percentages. One hundred percent plus 10 percent or one plus point one. One hundred and ten percent or one point one zero. And we're going to take that to the power of N negative in which is the number of periods or thirty five. So one hundred and ten percent or to the power of thirty five gives us about taking into consideration rounding. This is an excel.

Therefore the actual numbers being used, even though it's rounded to three point five six. Then if we take that one minus the three point five six, that being the numerator, giving us the entire numerator. That being at the ninety six point four for about. So now we have the numerator allowed. Let's take a look at the denominator, which is I or the rate or rate 10 percent. So we'll take that 10 percent. And now we have the numerator and denominator as one number. So when we do that, then we like to divide them. So now we're taking the ninety six point four four divided by the ten percent. Gives us about nine point six for about a note. Be careful of the decimals and whatnot, converting from decimals to percentages.

And then we've got the sixty thousand here times this nine point sixty four, which gives us the five seven eight six forty nine fifty four. Note that if I divide this out, that amount that we have on the table would be nine point six four four one five nine, which is basically this number which is rounded, rounded to two digits. If I took it out to this many digits, that's how many digits we can look at. And we'll compare that to the table that we'll see later. So in other words, we would have to put in five seventy eight six forty nine fifty four in order to get, you know, sixty thousand a year at the ten percent discount rate for the thirty five years. Let's do that with an Excel calculation.

If you were to put this in Excel and we do have the Excel problem, if you want to practice that one highly recommended. We would say, all right, well, then that would mean that the rate here would be the rate of the ten percent then comma and we would take the number of periods. Thirty five comma. And then because this is an annuity formula, we would be picking up the payment amount of the sixty thousand, and then nothing's in the future value because that would be used for the present value of one instead of an annuity that once again gives us to five seventy eight six forty nine point fifty four, which is the amount we'd have to put in in a lump sum. Now in order to get the sixty thousand a year, if we have the rate at the thirty five percent for the thirty five years, let's do it with the tables table time.

Same thing with the table time. Sixty thousand. We're going to look up on the annuity table making sure that we're picking up the correct table, not the table of one, but the present value annuity table this time. And we're looking at the thirty five and 10 percent. So 10 percent. Thirty five got the right table. So ten percent. Thirty five years. That's going to be the nine point sixty four for two. So there's the nine point six four four two from the table. Sixty thousand times to nine point six four four two gives us once again pretty much the same close to the same five seventy eight six fifty two. Why isn't that exact though? Because this is rounded to four digits this time and up top we use basically excel to calculate it, which took the full number even if we did round it. So notice, even if we're showing a number less than four digits, we actually use the whole number because we use Excel.

So be careful with that rounding. Get used to excel. Highly recommend using a spreadsheet. When you do so, you have to be careful of decimals, percents rounding. That's always, always the case. So we got the five seventy eight six five to this nine point six four four two is close to what we had up. Top here, we calculated it, if we took it out to more than four decimal nine points six four four one five nine. Note that in this problem, we actually only rounded it here to nine point sixty four. But this was actually done in Excel. So really, we're using the whole number in Excel. And and so that's what this number is going to be, the exact number, even though it's only showing the nine point sixty four.

And once again, get used to excel, get used to electronic spreadsheets. Know that concept because in practice, it's useful. So nine point six four four one five nine. And we have the nine point six four four two rounded to four digits result in this five seventy eight six fifty do being slightly different than the five seventy eight six forty nine. Also note that when you're talking about bigger numbers here, it's possible that rounding even four digits out might be slightly different. That will not be a problem. Normally for normal decision making purposes, it will be in material for normal decision making purposes. However, book problems can take advantage of that test. Questions can take advantage of that to force you to use one method or the other with regards to the multiple choice questions, which will simply differ by this in material amount, but which can distinguish the method that has been used to calculate it.

Future Value of an Annuity

Corporate finance practice problem within one note. Future value with uneven investments don't leave profits solely to chance. Instead, use corporate finance. Here we are in one note. If you have access to one note and would like to follow along, you're not required to. But if we'd like to, we're going to be in this tab on the left hand side, we're in the practice problems and then down in the 922 future value uneven investments. Here we are in one note. If you have access to one note and would like to follow along, you're not required to. But if you would like to. We're going to be in this chapter on this icon up top. We're practicing problems. We're down here at nine 22. Future value, uneven investments. Also note, if you're using one note, you might want to check out the immersive reader.

We will have some complimentary chapters down here with the text files that could complement having the same basic number and title as the practice problems. Those will basically be chapters, chapters that can then be translated using this tool to other languages. And you can actually play the audio in English, in other languages as a complement to this. This tab as well, closing this back up, is going to have our information up top. We will then do our calculation in the blue area down below. We'll do it in a few different ways. One with a mathematical formula. We'll also take a look at a running balanced type of calculation, possibly an Excel kind of format, how you might put it into an Excel type of calculation and then use the tables. Now we're looking at a future value type calculation here.

And normally when we break down these present values into future values or let's just think about future value at this point, we then have the future value of one or the future value of an annuity. But we can think about situations where things become uneven or things are not uniform in terms of a fixed number of payments or fixed interest rates. And then we'd have to break down our calculation or our projection into more detailed projections. This becomes burdensome to do if you don't have something like Excel, but with something like Excel, it becomes a little bit easier to do. We just have to visualize how we can then use our tools here, our future value tools to break down more complex types of scenarios.

So, for example, we have the original investment in this scenario being fourteen thousand for ten years, and then the percent is going to be 11 percent for those 10 years. Then we're imagining we take the proceeds from that after the 10 year investment, put them back in for another 12 years at 15 percent. So we have the future value of one. We don't have an annuity situation. We're not putting more money in each time, but we have a difference in the percentages that will come into play. Therefore, it's a bit more complex than just a future value of one. And we'll have to do basically two calculations in order to do it. So first, let's do it with a mathematical formula formula BEME.

Future value equals the present value times one plus R to the present value, then be in the fourteen thousand for the first line up. That will have to do first one plus RR being the 11 percent to the end, that being the period in this case, 10 years. We'll do it in a table format. We're going to break this formula out into, in essence, a table format. So we're going to put the PVG times, this whole thing in the water column and then calculate this detailed information in the inner column. So there's the present value of the fourteen thousand. Then we're going to take the one plus hour to the end. So we have the one plus R is 11 percent. And if I add those up, we get one hundred and eleven percent.

Be careful with the decimals, because again, if you did this in a calculator, you would, Of course, be doing something like one plus point one. One converting this to a percent would be one point one one. And if I convert that to a percent, it would be one hundred and eleven percent. So then we're going to take that and we're going to take it to the power of ten. So you're going to need some kind of calculator that has the ability to go to the power of the ten. If you do that in the computer calculator here, Windows calculator, let's go ahead and pick this up. We have a scientific calculator so we can then say there's going to be one point, one one, and then this is to the power of ten. And that's going to give us about if I move to make it a percent against the two eighty four about. And this is rounded right here.

This is the actual number up top. If we take that then and we multiply it times the 14 142000, then we get about this thirty nine seven fifty one eighty nine. So take into consideration rounding as we go with those calculations. I probably won't do the full calculation in the future, but make sure you have a calculator that you could do that to the power of 10 with and be careful with the percentage in decimal conversion. So now we're going to take that amount and then do our second component. So now we're at the end of that time period. We have got another present value of one, in essence for another 12 years. So for 12 years from that point in time is what we think.

Now, we're going to do our same kind of calculation, same same formula here, but starting at this point for the second component. So now we're going to pick up that thirty nine 752. This is rounded, noted, and then we're going to say that we have then the one plus hour to the end. So the one plus hour is now 15 for the second time period. So that's going to be one hundred and fifteen percent or one point one five. And then we're going to take that to the power of 12, to the power of 12, the number of periods. That's this and up top. And if we take that to the power of 12, we get about five thirty five notes I can take into consideration rounding here. And then if we multiply that out, the thirty nine seven fifty two times that five thirty five, we get the two one two six eight to fifty seven. So that's one way we can do it with a formula.

We can also, Of course, do it with a running balance table. Maybe not, Of course, do it with a running balance table, but you could do it with a running balanced table as well. And this could be tedious to do by hand without an Excel worksheet, but quite easy to do with an Excel worksheet. I highly recommend taking a look at the Excel worksheet. To do that, we do have the practice problem for it, and it gives you a lot more detail on the calculation. So we can say, for example, this first half here, we're going to say in period zero, I'm just going to name it, period zero to 10 at period zero. We started at fourteen thousand and then we took that 14. And let's plug that fourteen here, fourteen thousand times point one one.

Now we have one thousand five forty. Adding that to the original fourteen thousand we now have fifteen five forty. And then Of course we could take that amount and we could say let's multiply that times are rate point one, one that's going to give us our seventeen oh nine about its rounded plus what we had before, which is the one five five four zero. And that's going to give us our seventeen to forty nine. And then if we go to the next one, we could see how it's growing here. We could say those times the Times point one one and that's going to be the one eight nine seven about adding that then to the one seven two four nine point four we get the one nine one four six eighty six or about.

So let's go ahead. And if we do that all the way down, which again is tedious to do, like we're doing it by hand, but with Excel, you can use an autofill feature, which I highly recommend getting good at, because this type of running balance calculation is very useful and very easy and something that is worth understanding. So then if we get to this ending balance of thirty nine seven fifty one eighty nine, we can then go to a period, the next period out, which is our second calculation, just do the table again with our new rates. Now we're at period zero, which is really a period, you know, eleven after this after this time period and then go out twelve times up again, period. This is period zero period ten and then followed by the next time period.

So we're going to start here, do the same thing and we'll just take the thirty nine seven fifty one point eight, nine times the point one five this time instead of the point one one. And that would give us in this case, the five nine six three plus the three nine seven five one point eight nine. That gives us to forty five, seven, fourteen, sixty eight and so on and so forth. And we can get that running balanced. That would take us back down to one to six eighty to fifty seven. You can also see how this kind of scenario could lead us to make it easier for us to do more complex types of calculations. Because if I have this situation where I think the rate is going to change constantly, then, Of course, I can do this running balanced calculation and change the rates as necessary within it.

Not too difficult to do with Excel. So if we go back down again, let's try to do it again. Now, this is going to be with an Excel formula. We'll just kind of break down the Excel formula. Note that you can pick up the Excel formula in the Excel practice problem. This would probably be the most common way of someone doing this in practice type of problem using Excel or financial calculator in a similar way. So once again, we would have a formula down here. We're going to take the future value of one type of calculation and just plug this into our formula and just have it magically appear. So it would be the negative future value which will flip the sign of brackets. And then we got the rate. The rate would, Of course, for the first one, be 11 percent.

This would represent the number of periods, which would be the ten for the first one. Notice that we skipped over this item here because it's not an annuity. And if it were an annuity, meaning multiple payments, that would be here. We're just going to skip those two commas and go to the present value. And that'll give us once again our calculation for that first component, basically magically. And then we can go back down and do the second component where we do the same thing. The rate now is 15 percent. The number of periods is now going to be twelve and two commas, because once again, it is not an annuity. And then we pick up the present value, which is now this number, the thirty. Iron 751, and that once again will give us our magical end result, no.

This would most likely be the easiest way to calculate this, although the least transparent and just note how flexible these formulas are that we're using the present value in future value formulas of of both annuities and present value of one very flexible and useful formulas to be put into place if we can basically understand and visualize how and when to put them into place. We can then, Of course, do this with the tables down below. We have a similar type of situation. We would take the first amount at the fourteen thousand and look at the table and would say, we want 10 years, 11 or 11 percent and 10, 11 percent and 10 would be that two point eight three nine four. There's the two point eight three nine for the fourteen thousand types at two point eight three nine four is about thirty nine seven fifty one sixty.

Might be slightly different due to rounding due to this only going out for digits. Be careful of rounding. Then we could take that. Thirty nine seven fifty two. Now that's about our starting point. Go to the table and now we're looking at the 15 percent and 12 periods. So here's going to be the 15 percent. And the 12 periods would then be down here at the five point three five oh three. There's the five point three five oh trees that are thirty nine seven fifty two times the five point three, not five oh three gives us once again that two one two six eight two point nine nine could be slightly different due to the rounding that is taking place in these two calculations for these two percentages, taking them out only to four digits.

Future Value Uneven Investments

Corporate finance practice problem within one note. Future value with uneven investments don't leave profits solely to chance. Instead, use corporate finance. Here we are in one note. If you have access to one note and would like to follow along, you're not required to. But if we'd like to, we're going to be in this tab on the left hand side, we're in the practice problems and then down in the 922 future value uneven investments. Here we are in one note. If you have access to one note and would like to follow along, you're not required to. But if you would like to. We're going to be in this chapter on this icon up top. We're practicing problems. We're down here at nine 22. Future value, uneven investments. Also note, if you're using one note, you might want to check out the immersive reader.

We will have some complimentary chapters down here with the text files that could complement having the same basic number and title as the practice problems. Those will basically be chapters, chapters that can then be translated using this tool to other languages. And you can actually play the audio in English, in other languages as a complement to this. This tab as well, closing this back up, is going to have our information up top. We will then do our calculation in the blue area down below. We'll do it in a few different ways. One with a mathematical formula. We'll also take a look at a running balanced type of calculation, possibly an Excel kind of format, how you might put it into an Excel type of calculation and then use the tables. Now we're looking at a future value type calculation here.

And normally when we break down these present values into future values or let's just think about future value at this point, we then have the future value of one or the future value of an annuity. But we can think about situations where things become uneven or things are not uniform in terms of a fixed number of payments or fixed interest rates. And then we'd have to break down our calculation or our projection into more detailed projections. This becomes burdensome to do if you don't have something like Excel, but with something like Excel, it becomes a little bit easier to do. We just have to visualize how we can then use our tools here, our future value tools to break down more complex types of scenarios.

So, for example, we have the original investment in this scenario being fourteen thousand for ten years, and then the percent is going to be 11 percent for those 10 years. Then we're imagining we take the proceeds from that after the 10 year investment, put them back in for another 12 years at 15 percent. So we have the future value of one. We don't have an annuity situation. We're not putting more money in each time, but we have a difference in the percentages that will come into play. Therefore, it's a bit more complex than just a future value of one. And we'll have to do basically two calculations in order to do it. So first, let's do it with a mathematical formula formula BEME.

Future value equals the present value times one plus R to the present value, then be in the fourteen thousand for the first line up. That will have to do first one plus RR being the 11 percent to the end, that being the period in this case, 10 years. We'll do it in a table format. We're going to break this formula out into, in essence, a table format. So we're going to put the PVG times, this whole thing in the water column and then calculate this detailed information in the inner column. So there's the present value of the fourteen thousand. Then we're going to take the one plus hour to the end. So we have the one plus R is 11 percent. And if I add those up, we get one hundred and eleven percent.

Be careful with the decimals, because again, if you did this in a calculator, you would, Of course, be doing something like one plus point one. One converting this to a percent would be one point one one. And if I convert that to a percent, it would be one hundred and eleven percent. So then we're going to take that and we're going to take it to the power of ten. So you're going to need some kind of calculator that has the ability to go to the power of the ten. If you do that in the computer calculator here, Windows calculator, let's go ahead and pick this up. We have a scientific calculator so we can then say there's going to be one point, one one, and then this is to the power of ten. And that's going to give us about if I move to make it a percent against the two eighty four about. And this is rounded right here.

This is the actual number up top. If we take that then and we multiply it times the 14 142000, then we get about this thirty nine seven fifty one eighty nine. So take into consideration rounding as we go with those calculations. I probably won't do the full calculation in the future, but make sure you have a calculator that you could do that to the power of 10 with and be careful with the percentage in decimal conversion. So now we're going to take that amount and then do our second component. So now we're at the end of that time period. We have got another present value of one, in essence for another 12 years. So for 12 years from that point in time is what we think. Now, we're going to do our same kind of calculation, same same formula here, but starting at this point for the second component.

So now we're going to pick up that thirty nine 752. This is rounded, noted, and then we're going to say that we have then the one plus hour to the end. So the one plus hour is now 15 for the second time period. So that's going to be one hundred and fifteen percent or one point one five. And then we're going to take that to the power of 12, to the power of 12, the number of periods. That's this and up top. And if we take that to the power of 12, we get about five thirty five notes I can take into consideration rounding here. And then if we multiply that out, the thirty nine seven fifty two times that five thirty five, we get the two one two six eight to fifty seven. So that's one way we can do it with a formula. We can also, Of course, do it with a running balance table.

Maybe not, Of course, do it with a running balance table, but you could do it with a running balanced table as well. And this could be tedious to do by hand without an Excel worksheet, but quite easy to do with an Excel worksheet. I highly recommend taking a look at the Excel worksheet. To do that, we do have the practice problem for it, and it gives you a lot more detail on the calculation. So we can say, for example, this first half here, we're going to say in period zero, I'm just going to name it, period zero to 10 at period zero. We started at fourteen thousand and then we took that 14. And let's plug that fourteen here, fourteen thousand times point one one.

Now we have one thousand five forty. Adding that to the original fourteen thousand we now have fifteen five forty. And then Of course we could take that amount and we could say let's multiply that times are rate point one, one that's going to give us our seventeen oh nine about its rounded plus what we had before, which is the one five five four zero. And that's going to give us our seventeen to forty nine. And then if we go to the next one, we could see how it's growing here. We could say those times the Times point one one and that's going to be the one eight nine seven about adding that then to the one seven two four nine point four we get the one nine one four six eighty six or about.

So let's go ahead. And if we do that all the way down, which again is tedious to do, like we're doing it by hand, but with Excel, you can use an autofill feature, which I highly recommend getting good at, because this type of running balance calculation is very useful and very easy and something that is worth understanding. So then if we get to this ending balance of thirty nine seven fifty one eighty nine, we can then go to a period, the next period out, which is our second calculation, just do the table again with our new rates. Now we're at period zero, which is really a period, you know, eleven after this after this time period and then go out twelve times up again, period. This is period zero period ten and then followed by the next time period.

So we're going to start here, do the same thing and we'll just take the thirty nine seven fifty one point eight, nine times the point one five this time instead of the point one one. And that would give us in this case, the five nine six three plus the three nine seven five one point eight nine. That gives us to forty five, seven, fourteen, sixty eight and so on and so forth. And we can get that running balanced. That would take us back down to one to six eighty to fifty seven. You can also see how this kind of scenario could lead us to make it easier for us to do more complex types of calculations. Because if I have this situation where I think the rate is going to change constantly, then, Of course, I can do this running balanced calculation and change the rates as necessary within it.

Not too difficult to do with Excel. So if we go back down again, let's try to do it again. Now, this is going to be with an Excel formula. We'll just kind of break down the Excel formula. Note that you can pick up the Excel formula in the Excel practice problem. This would probably be the most common way of someone doing this in practice type of problem using Excel or financial calculator in a similar way. So once again, we would have a formula down here. We're going to take the future value of one type of calculation and just plug this into our formula and just have it magically appear. So it would be the negative future value which will flip the sign of brackets. And then we got the rate. The rate would, Of course, for the first one, be 11 percent.

This would represent the number of periods, which would be the ten for the first one. Notice that we skipped over this item here because it's not an annuity. And if it were an annuity, meaning multiple payments, that would be here. We're just going to skip those two commas and go to the present value. And that'll give us once again our calculation for that first component, basically magically. And then we can go back down and do the second component where we do the same thing. The rate now is 15 percent. The number of periods is now going to be twelve and two commas, because once again, it is not an annuity. And then we pick up the present value, which is now this number, the thirty.

Iron 751, and that once again will give us our magical end result, no. This would most likely be the easiest way to calculate this, although the least transparent and just note how flexible these formulas are that we're using the present value in future value formulas of of both annuities and present value of one very flexible and useful formulas to be put into place if we can basically understand and visualize how and when to put them into place. We can then, Of course, do this with the tables down below. We have a similar type of situation. We would take the first amount at the fourteen thousand and look at the table and would say, we want 10 years, 11 or 11 percent and 10, 11 percent and 10 would be that two point eight three nine four.

There's the two point eight three nine for the fourteen thousand types at two point eight three nine four is about thirty nine seven fifty one sixty. Might be slightly different due to rounding due to this only going out for digits. Be careful of rounding. Then we could take that. Thirty nine seven fifty two. Now that's about our starting point. Go to the table and now we're looking at the 15 percent and 12 periods. So here's going to be the 15 percent. And the 12 periods would then be down here at the five point three five oh three. There's the five point three five oh trees that are thirty nine seven fifty two times the five point three, not five oh three gives us once again that two one two six eight two point nine nine could be slightly different due to the rounding that is taking place in these two calculations for these two percentages, taking them out only to four digits.

Present Value Annuity

Corporate finance practice problem in one note. Present value of an annuity. You want to find that corporation, exercise, corporate finance. Here we are in one note. If you would like to follow along in one note, you're not required to. But if you have access to it and we'd like to, you were on the tab on the left hand side, where in the practice problems we're down here in the 923 present value of annuity chapter. Note also when using one note, you might want to check out the immersive reader and we may have complimentary chapters or tabs in one note in the practice problems as well as in the text practice problems down here with the same numbers. They often have this chapter, which can be read in English.

You can also listen to it with this tool. You can convert it to multiple different languages and either read it in English and or Spanish in that tool as well. Going to close up this top tab. Then we're going have our information up top. We'll do the calculation for it in a table type format or a mathematical format, I should say. And then we'll do a running balanced type of situation, breaking down the annuity to present the value of one calculation, which is a critical skill to have one a little bit more difficult to do without Excel. But if you have Excel or some other spreadsheet, it's very easy to do. We'll take a look at the Excel format for it to do the calculation as well, and then we'll do the table calculation as well. So going up top, we've got our new here. We're going to receive it per year. We're imagining we're going to be getting eleven thousand per year.

So you could think about a situation where you won a prize or something like that, and it's going to be given in the form of an annuity or something like that. And the years are going to be eight years. We're going to do this for the period of eighteen. We're going to assume the rate of 14 percent. We would have to determine that rate. Of course, in practice, that's going to be one of the unknowns that we don't really know that we need to figure out in order to do the calculation. So if we were just going to think about how much money we would either get in like a lottery or like if we won a prize, or how without any increase in value, the 11000 at times 18, we would have the one 98. Now, let's do the calculation for an annuity. Taking into consideration the 14 percent, our formula is going to be up top.

That's the first time. That's the first way. We will take a look at that. That's going to be P times one minus one plus R to the negative in overall. I'm going to put this into a table type of format, as I do so. And I do recommend practicing this in Excel. I know this is a little bit more unusual than something that you might do in a classroom where you're doing something in paper and pencil. You would write this down algebraically, but putting together tables like this is useful to do. If we want to break down this formula into a table, it's useful to do in practice. You would take the Vampi times, this entire column here, and then we're going to break out the numerator in more detail in the inner columns as well. So I'm going to take P.

It's going to be first in our table. We're then going to be taking a look at one. I'm going to pull into the enter column here for the numerator, and then we'll take a look at the one plus R to the negative end. So we're looking at the numerator now, one here in this column, and then we're going to break out in the inner column, one plus R to the negative in. So one plus R, 14 percent is one hundred and fourteen percent. Be careful about the decimals and the percentages. If I do this in a calculator it would be something like one plus point one four. It's going to be one hundred one point one four or one hundred and fourteen percent if we move the decimal places to places over. We're going to take that to the negative end.

Note that if you're going to use an Excel calculator here I'm sorry, a Windows calculator in our computer Windows operating system calculator, we have a scientific calculator that allows us to do that. And so we take the one point one four, and then we're going to hit the carrot up to the power of it. And I'm going to say eighteen and make that a negative with this little item down here, the negative eighteen and then equals. That gives us about the point oh nine four five six, one one and so on and so forth. And then we're going to take that. And now we've got this one minus that amount. So if I pull over the trusty calculator, we're going to start right now, take into consideration the rounding that we have here. Let's go back to the normal calculator, normal calculator, and then I'll make it a little smaller.

And now we're going to take the one minus the point zero nine four five six one one three five. And that gives us about this number here. And then if I go back down again, now we have the numerator and denominator as one number will divide those two out now. So we're going to take that and divide it by the point one four, which is the rate. And that's going to give us then our six point four, six, seven and so on about taking that then now we've. Pipi up top times that, so we're going to multiply that times the eleven thousand times the eleven thousand that's going to give us seventy one one forty one sixty three about. Now note that this number right here is basically the number that we would expect to see in the tables when we use the tables, although the tables will then use that in calculated out to only three or four digits, making it a slightly different result.

So if we go back down, we could do a similar kind of process of this then is going to be the seventy one thousand one forty one compared to you can kind of compare that to how much we actually put in or how much money we would get. Eleven thousand times the or four times the eighteen, which would be the one ninety one or one ninety eight thousand. So it would be one ninety eight thousand for the actual payments valued then on the present value at the seventy one 141. Sixty three due to the annuity type of payments. Let's calculate this down. And this is a useful tool to have as well, is to take that idea of an annuity payment, which is something that we can't simplify down to an annuity due to the fact that it is even payments.

But if we can, then we can also think about an annuity as 18 series of present value of one calculation's, which would be quite tedious to do if we were doing it with a mathematical formula, which is why the annuity is useful. But if we have excelled and we use the Excel formulas, it's easy for us to make a running balance table with this. And when we make more complex type of scenarios such as this scenario, if this were an investment, for example, where we put we put different amounts in in the future, instead of having it fixed at 11, we're going to put 11 for five years, and then we'll put like twelve thousand and then we'll put like fifteen thousand.

Then we have a more complex scenario and we cannot use an annuity calculation for the entire thing, but we can easily break it down to a present value of one calculation for the entire thing and or use some type of combination between the annuity calculations, where applicable and the present value of one calculation. So it's really useful to be able to visualize that. Once you understand the calculations, you can use something like Excel in order to apply the proper calculation. So if we were to do this, I'm going to imagine that we're using a financial calculator or excel to get to the present value calculation, and then we could basically just run our periods. I'm going to run from periods one down to period 18 and do our calculation here.

We would then say that payment is the eleven thousand originally put in if it's going to be put in a year from now. We can do a normal present value calculation, not an annuity calculation. I won't do it here. We're going to imagine we're doing it in Excel or a financial calculator, but we can do the present value of one calculation, with the difference being that I'm not bringing it back 18 periods. I'm only bringing it back one period, because I'm going to have the transaction each time period. So that's going to be then valued at the nine six four, nine, 12 about. And then in period two, we're going to have another 11000 that we're going to put in because it is an annuity.

We can then do a present value of one calculation, and we could take that one and bring it back to periods back to the current day. So obviously, the present value would be lower than the present value of the first payment that we put in there just one year out, whereas this one's two years out. And then if we take that nine, six, four, nine, 12 plus the eight, four, six, four, we get to the 18 one one three point two seven. If we continue on with this, Of course, then in the third period we put in another 11000. If we do a present value of one calculation, which is quite easy to do in like an Excel format, which we'll do in a practice problem, highly recommend taking a look at it, then we're going to get something that's going to be slightly lower again, because the periods that we use this time, we're three years out instead of one or two or eighteen.

And therefore, if we get something a little bit lower, if we take the 18 one one three point two, seven plus that seven, four to five, we're now to the twenty three, five, thirty seven, ninety five and so on and so forth for 18 periods. And then at the bottom line of this we get to the seventy one 141 sixty three, which is the same as the amount we got here. Seventy one one forty one sixty three. Now you might say why in the world would I do that when I can just do the annuity formula? Well, one, it gives you a little bit more transparency. It tells you what is actually happening in the running balance type of format. And Antu, like we see if any of these payments become uneven, say payment five here, you're imagining that if it's an investment, we're going to have more money.

We're going to put like fifteen thousand in at this point in time. Well, then you can do that a couple of different ways. You can use this running balance calculation and then just change the payment at this point to 15. Or you can use an annuity for the first four periods because it'll work for the four periods. And then in period five, you can have two. Switch things up, possibly because that's where you're going to have an adjustment to the payments that you'll have at that point, so you could have some combination in a more complex scenario of annuities for part of the complex scenario and present value of one, possibly four part of the scenario.

And if there's a problem at any point, if it's a complex scenario, you can always break it down to present the value of one calculation, even though, you know, it becomes a longer, more exhaustive thing to look at. And then you can combine them together where an annuity formula would fit and try to find the combination that would work best for your analysis, as well as the chapter type of analysis. If you're trying to explain something complex like present value investments, long term investments or long term planning to somebody else. You can also do this with, Of course, the annuity calculation down here. So this is just what we will do in Excel.

Highly recommend taking a look at Excel, but just a quick look at it. We can magically get the answer. Was something like this similar to a financial calculator, which would be equal to negative present value? We're going to use the same present value as whether it's annuity and annuity or a present value of one. We would then take the rate here in our calculation, which Of course, would be the 14 percent. We're talking years now if it was in months. Be careful because you'd have to divide that by 12 for the month's number of periods then 18. That's where the three would be. And then we're going to say the payment amount is going to be 11000. We use the payment amount in this calculation because it is an annuity.

If it were a present value of one. We would put a zero there or just two comments and then the future value, this being an annuity. We use that format. Notice that that allows us to use the same present value calculation for the present value of one present value of an annuity, just alter in between whether we're using this payment or the future value component of it. That, once again, Of course, gets us to the magic result of this number. Note most people, when you're talking to people that are dealing with some financial situation, magically put this number in and they get to this balance and they don't really possibly have a real understanding of what the balance is or how they got there or anything like that. And so it is useful to have to think about things in terms of a more complex, basically a table of items that have it and be able to think about how the present value of one is similar to the present value of an annuity and whatnot and all that kind of stuff.

And then if we do this with a table, same kind of thing with a table, you just gotta make sure you pick it up at the proper table, which would be the annuity table. Now, we have 11000. We're looking for 14 percent, 18 periods. So we got the 14 percent here, 18 periods is going to be down here somewhere. There it is, six point four, six, seven, four. So there's the six point four, six, seven, four. Once again, calculating out to the Seventy-One one forty one forty. This is not as exact as this number. Those two numbers are different, however, there is a small amount of difference.

Therefore, the table is probably good for normal types of decision making. It is rounded because we can see, Of course, the table is rounded to four digits. That's what's resulting in the difference. Make sure that you're aware of that. And if someone is asking a test question, for example, is asking about these calculations, they may force you to round the calculations to a certain decimal to try to force you to use whatever method that they are trying to get you to use. And you need to be aware of that so that you get to the proper number and find the right answer on the Excel sheet. Obviously, either method would be close enough, most likely for most normal in practice Decision-Making purposes.

Present Value Annuity Part 2

Corporate finance practice problem with one note, present value of an annuity. Get ready, it's time to take your chance with corporate finance. Here we are in one note. If you have access to one note and would like to follow along, you're not required to. But if you would like to. We're going to be in the icon on the left hand side in the practice problems area and down here in the nine at twenty six present value of an annuity. Also note, if you're using one note that you might want to take a look at the immersive future. Many of the chapters that we will have will then be mirrored down here in the text area. The text area will, in essence, be the chapters. The chapters can then be translated into Spanish and you can actually hear them and or read them in multiple languages with the use of the immersive reader to also check that out if it sounds interesting and close this back up.

Here's going to be our information up top and we are going to do the calculation a few different ways. We're going to do it with a present value. Mathematical type of calculation will then break down the annuity into the present value of one calculation is a really useful skill to have, and it's really necessary once you get into more complex types of scenarios that we will practice that again. And then we have the present value using Excel formulas, the easy way to get there, and then we'll do the present value with the use of the tables. So we're going to be running another kind of scenario here with our present values.

This time, we're going to say that we're going to receive imagining this like out, like if we want a prize, like a lottery or something like that, and they say you're going to be receiving so much money. And then in the fine print, you see that it's going to be in the format of an annuity, which is kind of deceiving, almost dishonest. But you say, OK, what if the prize, how much would we get here? We would say if we were getting forty thousand for 14 years, forty thousand times fourteen. So the prize might say that someone won five hundred and sixty thousand in a lottery or something like that in this type of scenario. And then you'd have to say, well, wait a second, the fine print says, yeah, but you don't get paid that in one lump sum. Today we're going to basically give it to you in forty thousand dollar amounts yearly. Again, that's still good.

I wouldn't complain or anything about it, but it's still a little deceiving because they say that they won five hundred and sixty thousand. That's not really true, because in present value dollars, that's not how much you would get. So similar scenario with an annuity as to what if we were going to put forty thousand dollars into, say, an investment account, where would we be at the end? What would be the value of the investment situation? And in other words, we could think of the present value of a series of payments we might put in and how much that would be equivalent, as if we were to put in, you know, the same dollar amount basically at this point in time in order to do the annuity type of calculation. And we do need a standard amount of payments here.

So the standard payment is in the 40 that allows us to instead of doing 14 present value calculations to do basically an annuity calculation, given we have uniformity in the payments as well as the percentage here. Now, if we do not have uniformity in some more complex scenario, then we can, Of course, do some type of combination between the present value of an annuity and the present value of one. We'll take a look at that when we get down to the second component of this. When we do basically break this down into multiple present values of one type of calculation. So here we go. We've got to break this down into a mathematical formula. First, we got the formula of T times one minus one plus R to the negative end over R.

That's going to be our calculation. We're going to break this down into basically a table type of calculation useful to be able to put an equation into a table in the water column. We're going to want to then have the P times, this whole thing. And then in this inner column, we're going to want to have the numerator and denominator broken out. And then in this inner column over here, we're going to further break out the numerator, given there's a lot going on with it. So we're going to save the payment which is going to be forty thousand. And then we're going to say that we're going to pick up the one. Now, going into the numerator minus, and then I'm going to break out this other kind of component into its own category one plus or to the negative end.

So then we're going to have in the inter column here one plus R, which is 14 percent too. And if we add them up, then one plus 14 percent. I'm going to pull up the trusty calculator, be careful of the decimals and percentages. So one we could represent is just one plus point one. Four would be one point one four or one point one or one 14 percent, whichever way we want to present that. And then we've got to take it to the negative DN, which is 14. This is the number of periods we're going to do a different calculator here, I believe, to be able to take it to that power. Let's change our calculator in windows to a scientific calculator. We're going to calculate scientifically here. So then I'm going to take this one point, one four.

And then we can take this to the power of. Which is the carrot up top 14. And I need to make it a negative, so I'm going to hit this little item down here to make it a negative and then calculate that we get about the point one five nine seven zero nine. So on and so forth. So there we have that. We subtract that from one then, because now we're up top here. So now we're going to take this one minus that. That will give us the full numerator. We've finally got to the numerator once we do this. So I'm going to take that minus one, and that's going to give us the point eight four zero two nine and so on. It's not negative because it's really one minus that number. And there we have that number. And then we're going to pull in the denominator here.

So now we got the numerator pulling in the denominator, which is 14 percent. So then we could take this number. It's negative here, but it's a positive number note for our purposes. And we're going to say divided by the point one four. That's going to give us about six points of two oh seven and so on, which I'm going to pull outside here. So now that's outside. So now we got our 40000 times this whole thing that we've now calculated. So. Forty thousand where we started. Times. This whole thing. So I'm going to take that whole thing. It's negative. But just note that it's you know, that's it's going to be a positive number times forty thousand forty thousand. And there are two four zero eight two point eight six about. And so that's what we have. So we had our forty forty thousand payments.

Remember, if we were just to think about the amount of the payments, I'm going to bring this back on over to our normal calculator and make it smaller. If we have just the normal payments, we would have the forty thousand, but we're going to get them over 14 years, which would be five hundred and sixty compared to if I was to present the value with the annuity. The two hundred and forty thousand eighty two. Eighty six is what we would have for the present value of it. So then if I go back on down, we're going to say. And also just realized that if you have an option of taking the current amount or taking some amount in the future, then that would be one of the calculations you would have to think about.

One of the varying factors, Of course, being the 14 percent. You have to come up with an appropriate percentage, which is going to be some type of estimate to think about what that should be. So present the value of an annuity. So now we're going to say that let's look at this in terms of breaking the annuity down into a single present value type of calculations. This is something that you could do in Excel. Highly recommend doing it in Excel. We do have this practice problem in Excel for you to work it there as well. Now, the reason this is really useful to do is because you should be able to see that when we break down an annuity to a present value of each period, 14 periods of present value calculations.

Then when we get to something that's more complex, not uniform, we have something that varies. In other words, between the payments that are happening and the percentages, possibly, then we can use some combination of present value of one calculation and present value of annuity calculations to maximize whatever we're doing. For us to see it as simply as possible and for us to explain it as simply as possible to somebody else. So we'll break this down here to 14 present values of one calculation, which would look something like this. If this first forty thousand was going to happen in a year or something like that, we would have to bring the forty thousand back to the current time period.

So we're taking this one payment, not 14 years out, but the one that's happening one year out and bringing it back with a present value formula, not present value of an annuity, present value of one. When we add up all those present values, then it'll add up to basically the same thing that you would get with the present value of an annuity, given the fact that we have standard payments and percentages. So if we brought this one back, I won't do the calculation here, but we assume we just do it in Excel. And it's a present value calculation. Then we're going to say that we start off with thirty five 087. Seventy two if we have the second payment that happens after the second year.

Now we're going to do a present value calculation at this time, not for period one, not for 14 periods, but for two periods, because this is that period two calculation. Bringing the forty thousand back to the present, Of course, the present value then being something different, something lower than the present, the first payment in terms of today's dollars. And then if we take the thirty five thousand, it's thirty five thousand eighty seven seventy two plus the thirty thousand seventy seven nine about that's rounded we get the sixty five eight sixty six forty two. And if we did this again, we got the present value of the third payment, another forty thousand present value calculation of that forty thousand this time using the number of periods of three as opposed to two, one or fourteen as we did before. And that then gives us another present value, slightly lower or lower than the prior two, because, Of course, that forty thousand will be received further into the future.

Therefore, further discounted. So the. Twenty six, nine nine. Nine added to the five eight sixty six forty two gives us the 90 to eight sixty five, twenty eight and so on and so forth. And then if we get down to the bottom of this, if we were to add this whole thing up, we get down to once again the two forty eighty to eighty six, which matches up to the two forty eighty to eighty six up top. So nope, if you look at this, it looks a little bit complex, but it does give us a lot more detail as to what is happening from period to period. And once again, realize that if you have something different, something different with regards to the standardization or less than standardized payments for a certain period of time, for example, within this 14 year time period, maybe you're getting uneven, you know, payments more in one period than another.

So you might have to use the present value of an annuity for maybe four years, and then the payment changes or something like that for a more complex payment situation or the percentage changes to some degree than you might have to say. Well, so many years out, I think the appropriate rate to be using would not be 14, but some other rate. Then once again, you might say, well, whenever it's standardized, if it were standardized, for example, for four time periods, then I can use an annuity for those four time periods and then possibly use the present value of one or some other annuity calculation for the future periods. So realize that you can always break it down, in other words, basically to a present value of one type of calculation.

But if you have a really long scenario of what is going on, then you might want to then use the present value of an annuity for the portions that you can, the portions that are uniform for chapter purposes. And just so you can better understand it and then break out whatever you need to break out with the present value of one calculation. So that's going to be that useful tool to have. And then if you're going to break this out or record this just with a calculation, I function in Excel, which you could do similar to a financial type of calculator. Then you can have something like this which is listed here. We do this in Excel two. So you can take a look, take a look at that as well. So it would be a present value calculation. The rate would then be 14 percent. This is a yearly rate.

If it was a monthly type of calculation taken into consideration, you would have to divide that by 12 comma. The number of periods is going to be, in this case, 14. Once again, these periods begin in terms of years for our problem here, comma, and then the fifth the payment, because it is an annuity, we have a payment be in the forty thousand. If it were not an annuity present value of one calculation, we would use the same thing. But instead of having a payment, that payment would then be zero or just two commas, and we would then utilize the future value, considering it is an annuity, we don't utilize the future value. And simply put, the payment amount of the forty thousand that then again gets us to the two hundred and forty thousand eighty two eighty six eighty six. Yes. Then we have the table down below one more time on the table.

We can look this up on the table and do a similar type of calculation. We've got fourteen and fourteen. That makes it easy, 14 and 14. I can remember that 14 percent down to the fourteen periods, six points oh two one. So there's the six point oh to one. The forty thousand times six point 0002 one is 240 084 close to but not exactly to the to forty eighty two eighty six due to the fact that it's only rounded out four digits. If you wanted to see the entire number we calculated it up here it would be the to six point 0002 oh seven one five oh three. But it rounded it down to six points. 0002 resulting in a slight difference.

One probably would not affect your decision making for most normal decisions, but one test question could be used to force you to pick one answer or another with a multiple choice question, for example, and force you to use one method or another. So note that these two methods down here, probably this method up top, would be most used in practice. But it's kind of a magical method and it would be useful again in those if you have a more complex type of scenario, you could see where you might be able to use a present value type of calculation here in Excel and combine that with the present value of one calculation. If you had something that was less standardized for certain parts of the scenario, meaning less standardized in terms of a whole fourteen years with regards to the payment amount or the percentage amount and or the percentage amounts.

Uneven Payments

Corporate finance practice problem in one note. Present value calculation, where we have uneven payments, don't leave profits solely to chance. Instead, use corporate finance. Here we are in one note. If you have access to one note and would like to follow along, you're not required to. But if you would like to. We're going to go into this item up top. We're in the practice problems chapter and the 927 tab, the present value uneven payments. Also note that if you are using one note, check out the resource for the immersive . Oftentimes, we will have a matching set of chapters down here in the text files with the same numbers which will provide the information that can then be read audibly, or they can be converted to other different languages and either read or listen to and other different languages as a complement to what we have up top here.

So I'm going to close this back out. Our information is going to be up top. We're then going to calculate this a few different ways. One is going to be with a standard mathematical type of calculation, with a formula. In other words, then we'll break the annuity down into the present value of one type of calculations, and then we'll also calculate it with a table type of format as well, and possibly an Excel equation to consider how that would be done as well. So scrolling then back up top, we have a bit more complex of a scenario with a present value type of situation. We're going to be receiving one million nine hundred thousand, we are imagining, over the next 30 years, and the percent is going to be 12 percent.

But there's also a balloon payment at the end of this series of payments, and that's for the one thousand five hundred that breaks the uniformity. So that breaks the ability to use simply one formula, an annuity type of formula, present value of an annuity with this balloon payment. So we have to break this down in some way to different types of chunks so we can calculate now, because this item here has one basic balloon payment at the end of this. Then the most logical way to think about it would be to say, hey, maybe I would use an annuity for this first half of the 30 years, and then I'll have to use basically the present value of one calculation for this last component, the balloon payment.

That's how we'll calculate it first. Note that if it was different, if a different type of complexity, then again, you can typically use the present value of an annuity and present value of one calculation in order to break it out. We will take a look at breaking the annuity out into a present value of one calculation as well, 30 of them, and adding them together. Tedious thing to do. If you don't have Excel, but if you have Excel, something that can be done as well as useful to basically see it in that format, because once seen, you can see how you can break out any type of these problems into that combination, even if they're going to be more complex in a fairly easy way with the help and use of spreadsheets and formulas.

So if we then pick this up, we're going to say we can imagine this being like another kind of price situation where they might say, if I was to take these payments, one nine zero zero zero zero times thirty, that would be fifty seven million. Right. And then we would add the balloon payment of the one five oh oh oh oh, oh, oh. And so then we'd have the fifty eight five hundred again, the amazing prize to win. But again, in the small print, it's a little bit different. We're saying, hey, but we're not getting that today. So although it's still amazing, it's still a little bit possibly less than you would think, given the fact that if you got that money all today, it would typically be worth more.

Here we're saying you're not going to get it for 30 years at this amount per year. And then you have the balloon payment basically at the end, which is a way to really drastically that balloon payment is really a way to drastically reduce the present value of something, because that portion you wouldn't get for 30 years. So, again, it would still be obviously amazing if you were to receive that. But the advertising or the idea that it's worth fifty eight five today in today's dollars would be kind of a little bit deceiving. Now, you can also think of this as a scenario in terms of how much money could I put in basically today.

For example, if I wanted to get money back, how much of a lump sum present value would I have to put in to get, you know, basically one million nine for a certain amount of time and possibly then have one million five hundred at the end, maybe as like maybe as like a cushion in case, you know, if you were doing like a life expectancy type of thing in case I live longer, you know, than I thought or something like that, that would be a similar type of scenario. Different scenarios you can think of. I think the easiest one for us to visualize is that kind of a prize type of scenario. And here so let's go ahead and do this first with our mathematical formulas. We're going to start with a present value of an annuity for this top portion, and then we'll calculate the balloon payment with a present value of once the formula is going to be P times one minus one plus R to the.

Negative in over are we'll do that and break that formula out into basically a table type of format we want in the outer column P times, this whole thing, and then in the inner columns will break out this numerator and a bit more detail. So there's one million nine. Then we're going to take the one plus R to the negative N, we're going to bring up this one. I'm pulling this out to the inner column here, and then I'm going to pick up this one plus R to the negative end. So we'll pick up the one plus the rate, which is 12 percent. That's going to give us one hundred and twelve percent, remember? Be careful of the decimals. That would be one as in one plus three point one, two. That's going to be one point one, two or one hundred and twelve percent.

We take that to the power of thirty or negative thirty, which we would need a separate calculator, such as a financial calculator. You can find that on your Windows calculator, but with a scientific calculator like so. And then we'll take that one point one two to the power of and then we're going to say thirty and make it a negative with this little item. They're negative thirty and that equals about. Pulling this down about the point four zero three three three seven nine and so on and so forth, then we're going to take this now. We're here now. We took the one plus R to the negative one. We're going to subtract one minus it. I'm going to take it minus one, which will make it a negative, even though it shouldn't be negative.

But I don't want to retype that long. So I'm going to say minus one. And there's the point nine, nine or nine six, six, six, two, two about. So we're going to take that then. And then we're going to take the 12 percent. This number is now the numerator. The denominator is simply the rate or 12 percent. So I'm going to take that. Even though it's negative, it's not going to bother me. I'm going to take that divided by the point one to 12 percent. Now, we're at the eight point zero five five one eight and so on and so forth. We're going to bring that into the outer column here. And now we're left with just P times, this whole thing, which is broken down to one number. So I'll take that number, even though it's negative and say times the one nine zero zero zero zero.

And that's going to give us our 15, three or four eight four nine point point five for about. I'm going to break this back into a normal calculator here. The standard calculator. And so there we have it. So we've taken that series of payments, which that in and of itself would be if it was just the payments, one nine zero zero zero zero times 30. And if we present value because it's a series of payments, we're bringing it down here using the rate or discount rate of 12 percent. Now, we have to account for the second half of this, which is going to be that balloon payment, which you're going to get at the end of the 30 year period. We've got to bring that all the way back. Now, it's a present value of one calculation formula being present.

Value equals the future value, which is now going to be that one five, one million, five times one over one plus R to the end, or is going to be the 12 percent and 30. So let's go ahead and do that in our little table format. We're going to take the one million five, which is basically like the numerator here. Then we're breaking out. Then the one plus R to the N, there's one. There's the R 12 percent. That gives us one hundred and twelve percent to the power of 30. I won't do the calculation again, but be careful of the decimals and percentages and make sure you get a calculator that you can take to the power of thirty or use Excel. And that'll give us the twenty nine point nine five, nine, nine and so on or so forth.

And then we're going to take the numerator divided by the denominator, which will be the one five divided by the twenty nine point nine five nine nine and so on, which gives us about fifty thousand sixty six point six eight nine. If we were to take that number divided by the one thousand five, this is the amount we would expect to see on, say, a table format that we can take a look at. And we'll see you later. Now, if we add those two up, then meaning we're adding up the amount from the annuity, plus the amount from the single lump sum at the end. That gives us our fifteen three fifty four nine sixteen forty two present values. So that's going to be the first way we can.

We can do this. We can also think about this and say, hey, why don't I break this whole thing down, then into the present value of one calculation and we'll have three of them, plus the balloon payment. Thirty one for that balloon payment at the end. So this is another way that you can basically see this note that any annuity we have, we could break it down to the present value of one calculation and/ or some combination of an annuity and a present value of one. So if we did this, we could say, OK, this annuity, for example, period one, we're imagining we'll get this one nine like a year out. If I present the value, I won't do the calculation. But I imagine doing it in, say, Excel, and we do do this in Excel.

Then you can easily kind of do this calculation and bring this back in the period of one period as opposed to thirty periods, because we're just talking about that first payment, which would present value down to this one six, nine, six, four to eight fifty seven. If I took the second payment, then we would do the present value of one, this time taking the number of periods to be two as opposed to one or 30, because we're just thinking about the second payment, the present value then, although the payment being the same will be less because it's two years out and therefore less in terms of the current value, then if we add this number and that number, we get to this number.

And then if we take a look at the third payment, once again, the one million nine hundred and period three, if we present value it back out, then using the same formula, differentiating between the number of periods there's been three periods as opposed to to one or 30, we got a present value, which will Of course, be lower than the prior to our present values because it's further into the future. If I take the value before this, the three million to one. One. Oh. Own six point nine four plus the current present value, one million three fifty two, three eighty two. We get the current value four, five, six, three, four, seven, nine, and so on and so forth. We do this all the way through to the 30 payments.

Tedious to do if we did this by hand. But in Excel, you can just use the autofill feature to populate this table quickly and you can get a lot more detail in terms of what is actually happening. And you could see the value of the payments decreasing over time. And then at the end, we'd also have to tack on this last payment, the balloon payment of the one million five hundred thousand at period thirty, doing another present value of one calculation and taking the number of units or the number of periods to be thirty, which would bring that down to this fifty thousand sixty seven, adding that up to the prior balance we had from the basically annuity, we broke down into present value of ones being now fifteen thousand three fifty four nine six forty two.

That then matched what we got up top fifteen three forty one nine sixteen forty two and so on. So that's another way we can do it. This would be a tedious way to do it for this 30 year annuity. And obviously we could do a similar kind of combination and annuity and a present value of one. If we did this with an excel and broke it down to its easiest formulas in Excel or using a financial calculator. Then, Of course, we would simply do the financial calculator calculation for the 30 year annuity and then one for the present value of one, and simply add those two together so we can break this down into basically two formula type calculations. If we did this in Excel, the first one would be the present value of an annuity.

This is a good example of the difference between the present value of an annuity and the present value of one in Excel. Those two use basically the same functions, but have a difference between the payment and the future value. So this one, for example, would be the present value of the rate, which would be the 12 percent comma, the number of periods, which would be 30 comma, and then the payment, which would be used, because this is going to be an annuity of the one million nine hundred that would then give us the fifteen, three or four eight forty nine fifty four. Then if we took the present value of the last payment, this balloon payment, that would be the present value of the rate, which once again would be twelve comma.

The number of periods would be thirty here because this one was paid all the way out at the end. And then we have two commas, or you can put a zero here because there is no payment here, because we're not using an annuity. We're simply bringing back the present value of one. And therefore, we will then use the present value or future value, I should say, which is going to be that one million five hundred, which we're pulling back to the present, which gives us then that fifty thousand sixty six eighty nine. Adding these two together once again gets us in a much quicker and simple way to the answer of 15 million three fifty four, nine, sixteen, forty two. Then if we were to do this with the tables, same kind of thing with the tables we do the annuity calculation and then the present value of one for the balloon payment, but with the tables. So the annuity would be here.

Just got to make sure you pick up the proper table now. Annuity table versus present value of one. We've got one million nine hundred thousand looking on the table for 30 years, 12 percent, 12 percent, 30 years. So here's the present value of one, 12 percent. Thirty years is way down here at the eight point five five two. So there's the eight point five five two that gives us the fifteen, three or four eight. Oh, slightly different than what we saw up above, most likely due to the fact that it's going to be rounded out to four digits. Then the present value of one, we're picking up that one million five hundred thousand thirty years out. We're looking for the table, picking up the proper table, which is now a present value of one, which is going to be at 30 and 12 again.

So we're looking down here, the present value of one, which is down here, 12 percent. Thirty years is going to be here. It's going to be the point three point oh three, three, four. So point three, three, four, multiplying that out gives us the fifty thousand one hundred about what we got before, but slightly different due to rounding because the tables take this out to solely four digits. Then if we add up the fifteen million, three or four, a O plus the fifty thousand one hundred, we get the fifteen three fifty four nine eighty which is close to what we had up top fifteen three fifty four nine sixteen forty two. It's going to be different due to the rounding we had with these two calculations, using the two tables, taking that out only to four digits.

Note that since we have a very large dollar amount here, those differences could be larger in terms of total dollar amounts, differences still most likely in material for normal decision making purposes, but something that could be utilized for test questions, for multiple choice type questions, for example. You distinguish the method that you will be using, so be careful with test questions. They might tell you, I want you to round it to a certain area. They might tell you, I want you to use a table and then put answers that look to be materially the same for decision making purposes, but distinct enough to differentiate what answer you would get, depending on the method you used to get it.

Future Value of a Collectible

Corporate finance practice problem within one note. Future value of a collectible, don't leave profits solely to chance. Instead, use corporate finance. Here we are in one note. If you have access to one note and would like to follow along, you're not required to. But if you have access and would like to share in the tab on the left hand side where in the practice problems, and then down here in the nine to nine future value of a collectible tab. Also note that if using one note, you might want to take a look at the immersive reader. We will typically have a mirin chapter down here in the text files. Those will be the chapters.

The chapters can then be listened to in an audio format. They can also be translated to other languages. And both read and listen to in the other languages, therefore being a good complement to many of the chapters. So I'm going to then close this back up again. Our information is going to be up top. We're then going to work this problem down below in the blue area. We will do so with a mathematical formula. Then we'll do so with a running balance. Then look at an Excel type of calculation and then the tables. So we've seen a future value calculation before. One of the major differences now is just the context that we're going to be running it in this being an idea that we're going to be putting money into some collectible, such as a painting or like stamps or like collectible wine or brandy or something like that.

And then it's going to go up over time. Right. So if we put money into our painting of thirty five thousand, then we can estimate what we think the future value will be? Difficult thing to calculate here, Of course, because we don't know how much of a painting is going to go up. I would think it being more volatile than other types of investments. But when investing, we still want to try to figure out what we think is going to happen. So we're going to say over 14 years that there's going to be an 11 percent increase. And using that information, we'll do basically a future value calculation. It's going to be a future value of one calculation, because we invested in this case in one item.

I imagine it to be like one painting or something like that. And then we'll apply our future value calculation starting out doing so with the future value formula. So that future value formula is going to equal the present value, the thirty five thousand that we use to purchase the painting. Times one plus hour to the end are being 11 percent and being the time of 14. We're going to break that out into a table type of format. And so I'm going to take the present value time to one plus R to the end in the outer column, one plus R to the end, then calculated in the or column. There's thirty five thousand for the present value. Now we're going to calculate the one plus the R to the carrot end. So one plus R, which is going to be the 11 percent that's going to give us one hundred and eleven. When we put that in the trusty calculator, make sure that you're being careful of the decimals of one.

Plus, the point one one would be one point one, one or one hundred and eleven percent. Then we're going to take that number of periods, in this case years, that being 14, to do that in our calculator. We need some kind of I'm going to change this in windows to a scientific calculator, which provides us the capacity of calculating this. And so I'm going to do this again, it's going to be a one point one one. And then I'm going to say, bring this up to the carrot up top and fourteen. And that's going to give us about that four three one zero four four. So I'm going to say, all right, there's the four three one zero four four. It's in percentage formats down here. Move the decimal two places over. Be careful on how you're utilizing percentages and decimals as you go back and forth between the two.

So now that we have those two items, we can multiply these two out. Now, the thirty five thousand times this amount is going to be. I'm going to multiply this out to about thirty five thousand, one hundred and fifty eight, sixty five and so on. So there we have that scrolling so that means that that thirty five thousand future value after 14 years, if we have the 11 percent, we're saying it's going to be at a value that painting we're imagining or the stamp's or like the alcohol that gets better apparently with age. One hundred and fifty eight. Sixty five, forty three.

So then we'll go down here and let's see this in terms of a running balance, how much would it go up per year? So we're going to think about how much it would increase per year. Just think about it as a similar kind of situation as if it was money increasing it per year. This is something that is useful to do. And I'm going to go back to the normal calculator to do it. Normal calculator. Make it a little bit smaller. It's harder to do without a spreadsheet. But if you have a spreadsheet it is very useful to do. Book problems often do not concentrate on this, but in practice it is very useful to understand the concept, as well as get more insights that you might be able to use to make decisions on.

So we'll say the thirty five thousand is going to be the first period. We'll just do our running balanced calculation. Thirty five thousand times point one, one that's going to be the three eight five zero. If I add that to the original thirty five thousand, we're up to thirty eight eight fifty. If we take that thirty eight fifty, we multiply it once again times two point one, one for the second period. Now compounding on it, we now have the four thousand to seventy four about taking that and adding it to where we stood before that, which is the thirty eight five zero. We're at forty three one twenty three. Then we could take that once again and multiply it times the point one one and we could see it increasing the amount of interest increasing as we compound four thousand seven forty four, adding that then to the four three one two three point five gives us the forty seven eight sixty seven and so on.

And we could do this process all the way down for fourteen years. Tedious to do here with a calculator. Not too hard. Very easy. In fact, with Excel, I highly recommend practicing with that. We do have this practice problem and others in Excel that you can practice with that will get us to this one. Fifty eight. Sixty five. And we have down here the one fifty eight, sixty five once again. Then we have the Excel formula. This is just a mirror of the Excel formula. This is a similar kind of process that you might do in a financial calculator or in Excel. This is the quickest way to do it. It's kind of a magical way to do it. Right. We're just going to put the formula in there. So the calculation would look something like this.

We're going to say the future value, the rate in this area, which was before, which would be the. Make sure you're picking up the correct rate in terms of the rate per period. This in years, therefore, no change needs to be made. But if we're in months, for example, you typically have to divide by twelve commas. The number of periods once again in years would be the fourteen comma, because this is not an annuity. We will not have a payment. Therefore we have two commas or you could put a zero in between there, and then we will have the present value, which is the thirty five thousand, which will magically provide you with the one hundred and fifty eight sixty five, forty three. Once again, let's do this again, this time using tables, this time using the table time. So we've got the fourteen and the eleven percent will just look that up on the tables, making sure that we have the proper table future value of one table.

Here's the 11 percent. Fourteen periods, which is going to be the four point three one zero four. So four point three one oh four simply taking then the thirty five thousand times to four point three, one for providing us with the one hundred and fifty eight sixty four, which is about what we got in the last calculations, which was slightly different due to rounding last calculation being one fifty eight sixty five point four three versus the one fifty eight sixty four point oh due to this calculation only being rounded out to four digits, that been good enough for normal decision making. Obviously, if we're trying to think about the value of our collectable painting, it's going to be some type of estimate. And that will typically be in the realm of error or materiality for us. But remember that a question could get quite picky in terms of the decimals, even though they probably wouldn't matter so much in practice and decision making to try to force you to use either one method or another and test you on whether you have indeed done so.

Future Value of an Annuity

Corporate finance practice problem using one note. Future value of an annuity calculation. Don't leave corporate profits solely to chance. Instead, use corporate finance. Here we are in one note. If you have access to one note and would like to follow along, you're not required to. But if you would like to. We're going to be in this icon on the left hand side. We're in the practice problems chapter down here in the nine at 30 future value of an annuity tab. Also note that when using one note, you might want to take a look at the immersive reader. Many of our chapters that are in the chapter area will also be down here in the text areas. These areas have the chapters, chapters that can then be converted to other languages and both listened to and read in other languages, therefore being a good complement to many people for the chapters. Please check those out and tell us what you think about them.

So anyways, we got up top, we have the information up top. Then we're going to put this information into the blue area down below, doing a couple of calculations for it. We'll do the calculations with a problem format, mathematical type of problem format. We will then take a look at a running balanced type of format. Well, then take a look at an Excel, how Excel might calculate it, and then we'll take a look at the tables, some rounding it out with table time, doing the tables, which is going to be fun. So in any case, it's going to be the future value of an annuity, the information, the investment per period. So we're going to be investing per period for 12 years, in our case, the two thousand five hundred at eight percent of nine percent. And then we're trying to see where we will be in the future after this series of payments, which is an annuity.

We will do this first with the mathematical calculation. So we're going to save the future value of an annuity is going to be equal to P times the one plus the R to the N minus one over R P is going to be the payments that will have the and that's going to be the two thousand five hundred that goes in per period for twelve periods at the nine percent. And then we have one plus R, the rate being the nine percent to the power of N, that's being the period of 12 years in our case, minus one divided by R, which is, Of course, once again, the rate. So note that if we just think about the amount of money that would go into this, if we were to invest this in at the two five zero zero times 12, we would have in the thirty thousand. But we want to then consider and take into consideration the nine percent rate.

Note that the nine percent rate is, Of course, something that we would have to figure and estimate. That's something that's not unknown. We'd have to come up with that and estimate it projecting out into the future so that we can make an estimate. So we're going to break this out into a formula first. And the outer column in our table type of format as we break down this algebra is going to be the P times, this whole thing in the middle. Then we'll break out the numerator and denominator in this column, and then any further breakout will break out on the numerator in this column here. So we have the two thousand five hundred that are bumpy. And then I'm going to pull into the inner column, this one plus R to the N minus one, that being the numerator.

So we have one plus our which is nine percent. That's going to give us a subtotal of one O nine. If I was going to put that into a calculator, be careful of the percentages and decimals. One plus one. I'm sorry. One plus point O nine point zero nine plus one would be one point O nine or one hundred and nine percent. So then we're going to take that to the power of any number of periods. To do that, we need some calculator that allows us to put the carrot in there for the power of I'm going to change our Windows calculator to a scientific calculator, which I can then put this in there as one point nine to the power of. And then I put a little carrot there. There's a little carrot. Twelve, I want to make that. That's it. And enter. So we've got the two point eight one, two, six, six. So let's check that out.

Two point eight, one, two, six, six. So we have that. That's going to be this. Now I'm going to subtract the one. So minus one. And so if I take that, I'm just going to say minus one. And that's going to give us our one point eight one, two, six, six. So there's our one point eight one, two, six, six. And then we have now the numerator. The denominator isn't going to be the rate of nine percent. So nine percent once again. So I'm going to take this amount. I'm going to divide it by the point of, oh, nine, nine percent. That gives us about twenty points, one four oh seven. And so on, twenty points one four oh seven. So now we had this whole thing calculated in one number. We can now multiply it times P, which was up top in 2005. So we'll take that item again, multiply it times the twenty five two five.

Oh oh that's going to give us the fifty three fifty one point seven nine nine. And so on. So fifty three, fifty one, and then it's rounded to twenty eight. OK, so then if this item is right here, this is basically what we would expect to see, that twenty point one four oh seven on a table. So when we get down to the table time, this is what we expect to see, although the table will break it down into simply four digits most likely. And so it will be rounded slightly. Then going down, we can break this out now to a table. So let's think about this. In a running balanced type of table, this could be a little tedious to do in this format. But if you have access to a worksheet like Excel, then this is doable and useful to do. Going to change the calculator back to the standard calculator.

Make it a little bit smaller here. So if we were to run this out, then the first period we're going to say is two thousand five hundred, and then we're going to say then a year out. We're going to say that two thousand five hundred is going to grow by 12 percent. I'm sorry, nine percent point nine to be to fifty two hundred and twenty five. And we're going to put in another two thousand five hundred. So that plus the added to five hundred. It's going to give us that increase. Plus what was already in there of the original two thousand five hundred 225000. That gives us the five to twenty five. Now we can take that five to two to five, five, two to five times point zero nine.

And that's going to give us the four seventy four seventy and we put in another two thousand five hundred because this is an annuity 225000. So that's the increase plus what we had in there before, which was the five to twenty five that's going to give us the eight one nine five point two five. Once again, we could take that and multiply it times point oh nine again and that'll give us then an increase of these seven thirty eight about plus we're going to put in another two five zero zero plus two five zero zero. That's the increase plus what we had before, which is the eight one nine five point two five. That's going to give us the eleven for thirty two point eighty two. We can go on through this process.

And after the twelve periods, we would arrive at the fifty thousand three fifty one eighty then matching what we have up to the fifty thousand at 350 180. This table would be a tedious process to do by hand. But again, with Excel, this is an easy thing to make and it can give us a lot more insight in terms of what's happening as the interest grows over time. Let's go down to an Excel type of calculation, same kind of thing. But now we're going to be doing it in Excel, kind of a magic way as similar as you might do in a financial calculator. So within Excel, we'd have the future value calculation. And then you have the item down here. You would be picking up the rate, which would be the nine percent, and then the number of periods which would be 12.

You have to be careful making sure that you're lining up the rate and the period. Nine percent per year, years are what we're using here. If it were months, you divide by twelve for the the percent and then four years if it was, you got to be careful that you're using what periods you're using years or months and then comma and then we're going to be picking up the two thousand five hundred, which will be the payments, remembering that the payment item is what will be used when we use the same formula for the future value of an annuity, as opposed to if it was the future value of one item where we would not use the payment, but simply put, a zero or two commas and then use the present value.

So that's going to magically give us the fifty thousand three fifty one eighty and we could do this again, this time using the table. So we're going to finish it off with the table time down here, just making sure that we're picking up the proper tables. So we're going to take the amount of the payments to two thousand five and then pick up the amount from the tables down by making sure that we have the proper table that is in the future value of an annuity as opposed to the future value of one. Then we're going to say that we have V percent, nine percent, 12 B in the period. So we're going to say nine percent and 12 down here, twenty points one for one. So there's that twenty point one four one for the twenty five times.

The twenty point one four one gives us fifty thousand three fifty two point five, which is close to what we got before, which was the fifty thousand three fifty one point eight, slightly different Y because the table rounded in this case two, three digits. So that would be close enough for decision making purposes typically, but slightly different than what we had before. What would that percent be if they took out more than three digits? Well, we calculated it up top. I believe if we go back and on up top, it would be closer to the twenty point one four oh seven one nine eight and so on, which you could see calculated here, or you could see it calculated down here by taking the fifty thousand three fifty one point eight divided by the two thousand five hundred, once again, giving us that twenty thousand or twenty point one four oh seven one nine eight, as opposed to the three digit calculation, twenty point one four one taking that out to three decimals.

How Long to Double or Triple Investments

Corporate finance practice problem using one note. Future value calculation, asking the question of how long will it take before an investment doubles or triples, don't leave profits solely to chance. Instead, use corporate finance. Here we are in one note. If you have access to one note and would like to follow along, you're not required to. But if you would like to. We're going to be in the tab on the left hand side where there are practice problems. And then down here in number nine three one. Future value. How long do double or triple investments take? Also note that when using one note, you might want to check out the immersive . Many of our problems will be mirrored down here in the text chapter.

The text chapter has chapters that can then be translated into multiple other languages and either heard or read in those other languages, as well as English, thereby being a complement to the practice problems up top. So check those out if those sound useful and give us some feedback if they're helpful to you. We have our information that's going to be up top. We're going to calculate the information. Then down below on it, we'll do it using multiple different methods. Little bit different from the scenario here. So our question being, how long does it take for an investment to double or triple? Note that we don't really necessarily have to actually provide the investment, which is what would probably be done in practice.

We might say, hey, I got this much money. I want to know how long it would take for me to double my money if we assume a rate of six percent, for example. But we don't really need the fixed amount, the first amount, because you can basically provide it because it's going to take the same amount of time to pass. And we will just pick a number you could pick like one, we're going to pick a thousand to plug in. So we're going to say that we have a thousand dollar initial investment and then you could just work the algebra for it. So we would have a future value equation, which would be the future value equals the present value times one plus R to the N. We would assume that the present value would be one thousand our initial investment if we wanted to double it.

Then we could also assume that the future value would be two thousand doubling of the initial investment of one thousand. So we then would have a figure here for future value, for the present value. And then one plus r r is going to be the six percent. And then to the M end would then be the unknown. And then, Of course, we have one unknown. We could solve for the unknown. I won't go through the algebra for that here. I also just want to point out that you can do this in other different ways with the use of Excel as well, and show how that is applicable with the Excel formula. Let's first look at this mathematically as we have broken it down in the past.

So if we break down this equation to a mathematical equation, as we've seen it before and like a table type of format, we had the initial investment, which we said was going to be the one thousand that's going to be equivalent to this PV here. And then we had one plus six percent. One hundred and six percent. And then to the power of. That's the unknown in. So typically this yellow number then for our equation would be the unknown. And then this number we can basically derived, because the bottom line number down here needs to be two thousand, right. Because if this number is one thousand, the bottom line number needs to be two thousand.

So then our goal then, Of course, is to back into the number of periods. Obviously, this number right here needs to be two, because we know that one thousand times the two were two hundred percent would give us the two thousand. So if we then we're going to back into this item here. Note that we could, Of course, do that algebraically using our formula up top. But if you have something like this that would be in an Excel sheet and this is more transparent, which we actually could use the algebra. But if you're using a function like a future value type of formula function within Excel, it's more difficult for us to basically back into a different unknown within that same equation. What we can then do is use something like a goal, see if there's a goal feature, meaning in other words, if I had this calculated in Excel, I could basically keep changing this number here.

I could start with a fixed number like five or just pick a number and then try and error until I get to a number that's going to approximate what my end value will be. That's one way we can basically find the answer through trial and error. And we can do that with a feature on an excel, which I highly recommend going in and taking a look at. So that you can then practice using a feature like that. And it's called goal seeking to do that. Now, again, if we know the algebra for something, we can go ahead and solve the algebra. But it's useful to look at the algebra and see how you would do that. First, you would be basically just plugging in this number and letting everything else work out itself because you have a spreadsheet.

It could do that fairly quickly. And then you just tell Excel to basically do that for us using the ghostly feature. And then if we apply that same concept to something like a formula, I'm going to jump down here to the use of the formula. This would be us solving this. Problem basically with a formula. Now, this would be similar to what we might do in practice if I was to solve this in practice and say, OK, I have a thousand, I want to know when it's going to double. What I would like to use is this function in Excel to do it. So I may not even know what the actual formula is. I don't really need to know because I'm going to put in this function. It's going to give me the answer.

But this function, Of course, is to solve for the future value. And so and what I'm really looking for is the time frame, which is going to be the number of periods right here. So what I would want to do then is instead of me looking for another function in Excel, which is going to solve for the number of periods which they may have, but is far less common than the future value formula, I could still use this future value formula and use the same kind of method to solve for the one unknown. In other words, as long as there's still only one unknown here, I could use the same formula and go seek to do basically the algebra. But instead of doing the mathematical algebra of doing a trial and error format to find the figure that fits. So, in other words, if I was to fill out this formula, I'd say this is going to be the future value. The rate is known.

That's going to be the six percent, the number of periods. That's the unknown. So what do I put there when I start? I have to put something there. We can plug in some number that we can put into a formula down here, which would be like we can start with five or ten and then just put a random number there so that it can still calculate it and it can pick a cell on which you could change once we do the , and then we can put a comma and the present value would then be the figure that we gave the one thousand, then the unknown is really in this cell. And then what we can do is we can use this function, we can use goal seq, which I highly recommend taking a look at in Excel.

And that would be kind of the substitute of using algebra so we can use the same function, which is a more well known function than a function that could be in Excel, that would solve for the number of payments to then find another unknown, in this case being the number of payments. And then you could basically solve for that and they could find you then the number of payments in that format. Let's go back up top and look at it another way, this time with our running ballot's type of calculation. This is not something you would probably see in a book problem, but if you have Excel, you can do a running balanced type of format like this, a really useful calculation to do it.

So if we were to see this format, we could say, OK, let's start off with that one thousand, which we're saying that's going to be our original investment. And I'm just going to do this running balance until we get up to two thousand. So that's when it would double. So I'm just going to go period by period until we get up to two. So we just go, OK, we got the one thousand times the six percent point zero six, and that's going to be sixty dollars on the interest in the sixty dollars plus the original one thousand gives us to one thousand sixty that times these six percent times point oh six is going to give us the sixty point six sixty three point six or sixty four about plus the one one to three point six. And we would go on and so forth. This would be very tedious to do with a calculator.

But in Excel it is quite easy because we can use the autofill to do that. We do have this problem. And Excel Innisfail you might want to check. Take a look at that. And when we get down to cheer between 11 and 12, we can see, OK, now it clears. It goes past the two thousand in between there. So we know then that it's going to be somewhere between a period 11 and 12. If we wanted to break it down further, we can then say these are years that we're talking about in terms of the periods. So there's 12 months we can stay there.

So this one hundred and fourteen, if I take out one one four and divide it by 12, we could further approximate the information here by saying we're going to apply out for twelve months eleven to here, because that's going to clear over the two thousand and continue and continue on with our running balance. Now on a monthly basis. So after year 11, one eight nine eight point three plus your 11 month one nine point four nine would give us about one nine zero eight. And then I'd say plus another one. Another nine point four nine. And that would give us about one nine one seven. And so we could see that it's going to be somewhere down here on Allgier, 11 months between 10 and 11, 10 and 11 that we can kind of find it.

So you can use a running balance to kind of figure that out or at least approximate what it would be as well. Then the other way we could do this is with the tables, which, again, it's kind of like an approximation type of format. Tables would probably be best to approximate it. So we can then say we know if we start with the one thousand here that we have to end at two thousand in order to double it. And on the table, that would mean that we need to find two on the table, because one thousand times two would equal two thousand. We know what the rate is. The rate is. Going to be six percent. We just don't know the number of periods, so if I go to the six percent, I'm just looking for where two shows up and that's going to be down here somewhere between 11 and 12.

So we know that somewhere between period 11 and a 12 from the table is when it is going to go from one to two, and then we could get more approximations by those percentages. But that's another way that we can kind of approximate and back into the number of periods. So let's do it again. Let's say, well, what if it triples? If we do the same thing and say, OK, I need something to triple. We could do it with the formula and we could say, OK, the original investment, let's just make up a number, could be one, we're going to choose one thousand again. So we're going to say the original investment has a present value of one thousand, which would be PJV times one plus the area it's going to be six percent to the end is unknown. The future value is No.

One, because it's got a triple. And if we put in one thousand, triple in times three would be three thousand. So it would be three thousand equals one thousand times one plus R, which would be six percent to the end and then be in the unknown. We can work the algebra in that format or we could use the goal seek in a similar format. So I'm going to break the math down here into our table, as we've seen in the past, to discuss goal seek, which we probably wouldn't use in a formula like this as much, but rather in the Excel formula for the future value. So this is just, you know, that kind of a precursor to the use of the formula to see how it works.

So if we had the one thousand and then we have the one plus six percent gives us the one hundred and six, this would then be the unknown. We know that this number needs to be three thousand, because one thousand times that or three hundred three or three hundred times three would be the three thousand. So we got one thousand times. The three is the three thousand. This would then be the unknown if these were all connected with formulas in Excel. We can use trial and error to basically back in instead of doing the algebra and solving for N, we can simply use trial and error. And let the system then find it out.

Plugging in numbers, starting possibly with 10 and just going up from there until we get to approximately three thousand and using Excel, we can accelerate that by using Goldstrike, basically telling Excel to do that for us. So that's how we can derive this number and a formula basis. We would probably apply that more likely to something like a formula in Excel. So if we had something like this in Excel, then once again, I'm saying I'd like to solve for this one. The number of periods. But what I want to use is the future value type of formula, just like we do up here when we have this equation. Anything that I'm searching for that fits into this equation, if I only have one unknown, I can use this equation. We don't know in here if we know everything else. I have one unknown.

Therefore, I can search for it. But down here, I can't really do the algebra because it's a function in Excel. And if we have more complex functions, it can be quite complex to figure out what the function means in mathematical terms. What I'd like to do is basically use it in the same format, meaning I'd like to know if any of these are unknown. If I only have one unknown, then I'd like to be able to use this function. The way to do that is to use that trial and error format. So I could say that this is going to be the future value of the rate, which we know is going to be that six percent comma, the number of periods. That's what we do not know. So we make up a number first. I put it in another.

So I made up some numbers like ten. Put it in that cell and then comma, comma, and then the future value. I mean, the present value is something that we know because that's going to be one thousand. So we enter that. That's going to give us a result. What we want is for that result to reach three thousand. So what we would then do is use Goldstrike to change this number. We can keep changing this number using trial and error. So this formula then generates the number that we know it should be, which in this case is three thousand, thereby solving for the number of periods we could do that manually. And Excel doesn't take a whole lot of time, oftentimes manually, to do that.

But we can use goal seek to do that more quickly for us in that way, even though we don't have a mathematical formula to use algebra on. We can have the same concept using this format. And if there's only one unknown in it, use it in a similar way, finding that one unknown with the use of , which basically replaces the algebra with a trial and error kind of method to locate the unknown number. So actually quite a useful tool. So then we can use the tables, Of course, as well, to approximate. So if I start with one thousand, I want to end at three thousand because I want it to triple. That means the number on the table needs to be three. So I'm looking. Or six percent, something on the table that gives me three.

So if I go on down here six percent, I'm going to go on down to where it gets to three right here. That's between 11 and 12. So six percent I'm sorry, I'm not six percent. We need to get to three. That's two. Three. I got to count up to three. That's somewhere between 18 and 17, 18 and 19. So somewhere between 18 and 19 is when it gets to three on the table. So that would be an approximation of the period 18 and 19. We can then take a percentage of those and try to approximate, you know, how close in between those are. But that's one way we could basically use the tables. Clearly, the tables are a less efficient way to find this answer, but you could see kind of how it works, how you basically back into it with the use of the tables if you need it to.

Estimate Stock Returns & Sale

Corporate finance practice problem using one note, present value calculation to estimate stock returns and sale. Get ready, it's time to take your chance with corporate finance. Here we are into one note. If you have access to one note and would like to follow along, you're not required to. But if you would like to, we're going to be in the tab on the left hand side. We're in the practice problems then down here in the 933 present value estimate, stock return and sales tab. Also note that if using one note, you might want to take a look at the immersive reader. Many of our chapters will also have a text component down here with the same number that has the chapters. With this tool, the immersive reader, you can convert the chapters to multiple different languages and either read them or hear them in multiple different languages, making them a good complement to the chapters.

So check those out. And if they're useful, please give us feedback on that. Here we have the information up top. We're going to be calculating that information down below in a few different ways, a little bit more complex of a scenario we have. It's a present value type of situation. But now we have a situation where we're going to have investments. We're imagining basically stock investments here, and we're gonna have a return on the investments over the next three years. And then we're imagining we sell the investments. This could be a similar type of scenario for different types of investments that are going to be more complex than a fixed return.

So obviously, if we're putting something into, say, an investment where we're at, we're expecting a fixed return, then we can use a present value of one or annuity type of calculation for it if it's going to be a standardized system. But if the returns are going to be uneven, then we're going to have to do some combination of the annuities and present value of one. So here's a kind of an example of that. So, for example, if we put in an investment and expect after year one, we're going to get a return, let's say dividends on it of one hundred dollars and thirty four cents. Then we can present the value that if we have a year or two, we expect to get a return of one hundred and ten thousand forty seven year three, one hundred and sixteen, twenty one in terms of dividends coming back after the initial investment.

And then we expect to sell the stock after year three for one thousand fifty five. Obviously, these are all estimates. One way we can do this is we can say, OK, they're not even. Therefore, I'd have to present the value of each one of these taking this problem basically into making it into one to three, four present value types of calculations that we can then add up to get to the total number of what we believe the present value to be. Another method you might use is if these three items were more standardized, maybe I don't know what they will be for the next three years. And I will just estimate what I think the return will be in terms of dividends. Then I might use a uniform amount for these three items.

And in that case, we could still use the same method using a present value of the three of the four different cash flows. Or we can use basically an annuity, if these were all the same for these three calculations and annuity calculation and then a present value of one calculation for this item at the end. So note that you could usually break this type of calculation down to its present value components, and then the annuity would simplify things if you needed to. If you have Excel, then doing multiple present values is not that difficult. If you're doing them by hand, it becomes more difficult to do. So we'll do the calculations a couple of different ways. First, we'll do the formula, which will be the more complex way, and then we'll consider how that might be done using an Excel format and other types of formats as well.

So our calculation here, we're going to be doing four of these. So this will be kind of a long problem here. We're going to have the present value equals the future value of one over one plus hour to the end. We're going to start with this one up top, the one hundred, which is only a year out. So we put in an initial investment, expecting a return after the first year in the form of, say, a dividend of one hundred dollars and thirty four cents. Plugging this into our table type of format, we're going to say we have the one hundred and thirty four. That's going to be the future value. Then we have the one plus hour to the end. That's going to be one plus hour, which is going to be the 10 percent. One hundred and ten percent.

And we're going to take that to the power of NPS, which in this case is simply one, because it's one year out. So that's going to be the power of the end. We didn't have the one hundred point three or four times or divided by the one point one that's going to give us then the ninety one twenty two. So our return we expect to receive then is the one hundred thirty four, bringing it back to the current day from a year in the future to the present it being present valued at the ninety one twenty two. Then if we do this again for the second one, the one hundred and ten forty seven, plug this into our formula. Now we're two years out.

This is the return we expect after year two of the investment that's going to be the one hundred and ten. Then we've got the one plus R to the N. So we got the one plus the hour, which is 10 percent, 110 percent, if we add those up to the periods now to two periods out, two years out in our practice problem. So one hundred and ten to the power of two then gives us the one point to one. If we take the one hundred ten, forty seven divided by the one point two to one, that then gives us 90, 130. In other words, after year two, we expect to receive a return dividend. One hundred and ten, forty seven in dollars, but present value in those back to the current time period.

That's at ninety one dollars and thirty cents. Next we go to your three where we expect to receive a return of one hundred and sixty and twenty one. And then we expect to sell it for one thousand fifty five. I'm going to break these out into two separate calculations. We may be able to combine them together since they're both basically three years out. I'll break them out into two separate items. So the dividend then we're going to have the one hundred and and twenty one and same calculation here, one plus the 10 percent it gives us the one hundred and ten percent now to the power of three. So that's going to be one point three, three, one. We take the one sixteen twenty one divided by the one point three three one that gives us the eighty seven point three one.

So again, we're going to receive three years from now one sixteen twenty one, which if we bring the present value back to the current day would be the eighty seven thirty one. Lastly, we got the last one here. We're going to sell the stocks for one thousand fifty five. That's going to be in year three or after three years as well. So we got a present value, that one using the same method we did up top. So we're going to say that's going to be the one thousand fifty five and then the one plus the 10 percent. One hundred and ten percent. And then take it to the power of three again, which gives us eighty one point three, three one. So that one thousand fifty five divided by the one point three three one gives us the seven ninety to sixty four.

So we're going to receive in dollars one thousand fifty five after the three years when we sell our investment, the stocks in this case. And if we present value it, bring in those dollars back to be the current value that gives us these seven ninety two sixty four. Then if we add all this up for all these items we have, we got this seven nine two point six four plus the dividend for after three years, which was the eighty seven point three one plus and then the dividend after two years, which was the ninety one point three plus. And then we have the dividend after one year, the ninety one point two two. And that gives them about one or six to forty seven. Note that there is rounding going to be involved if we add those up. So there we have that.

Now, that would be the long, tedious way of doing it. If you had excelled, you can make this a lot quicker and you'd have the formulas that would look something like this. We're going to have just a series of the present value formulas, present value of one formula, not being able to use the annuity, even though there's multiple years involved due to the fact that there's inconsistent on ununiformed amounts of the payments that we're having. So it would look something like this. We've got this equals the present value of the rate. So the rate would be 10 percent, comma one. The first item up here is that one hundred would be for one one year out, one hundred thirty four, comma, comma, because it is not an annuity.

And then the future value here would then be the one hundred thirty four. That then gives us magically the ninety one twenty two. Then we would do a similar kind of present value for the second item that was for the one ten forty seven, which is two years out present value of the rate, which once again would be six percent comma. Now we're at two because this would be the dividend for two years out then comma, comma, because we don't have a payment, it not being an annuity, we take the future value, which would then be that one hundred and ten, forty seven that year to dividend. That gives us then the ninety one point three zero magically. Then we'll take the third one, the one sixteen twenty one do that again. Present value.

The rate would then be the six percent the number of periods now three because this is three years out then comma comma because there is no payment and then we have the future value which this time would be the one sixteen twenty one note that we might be able to combine these two together because they both happened three years out, even though there are different things, one being the dividend, the other being the sale. So then we would do that one more time for the sale. That would be the one thousand fifty five sale of the stock. The rate one once again, six percent number of periods, three again, because we sold it after the third year after we got our dividend karma. Karma, because there's no payment, because it's not an annuity.

And then the future value being that one thousand fifty five that gives us these seven ninety two sixty four. If we add this series of activities over the three year period, given the three amounts for the dividends and the one amount for the sale at the end we come to the one thousand sixty two forty six and we can then make a comparison of this result compared to possibly the initial investment put in. That we basically put in now, we're going to do a similar kind of process with the table, so we're at the table. Time now. So we have year one. We had the one hundred point three for the one hundred point three four.

That's going to be at 10 percent one year out. If we look at the tables and 10 percent one year out is going to be the point nine oh nine one. So there's three point nine oh nine one, which gives us the ninety one point two to then two years out, we have this one hundred ten point four, seven, one, ten, four, seven, 10 percent, two years out. So we got the 10 percent into 10 and two gives us the point eight to six four. So there's the point eight to six for us is the one ten forty seven times the point eight to six four gives us the Ninety-One. Twenty nine. And then we have the one one six point two one, which is three years out.

So let's take a look at that one. We've got the ten and three gives us the point seven five one three. So the one one six point two one times the point seven five one three gives us eighty seven thirty one. And finally, we have the one thousand fifty five sale of the stock that also happened in year three. Therefore, the one thousand fifty five times the same one. We don't even have to look at the table again because it's the same as the last one, because it's three years out. So that's going to be two point seven five one three. And that'll give us these seven nine two point six two adding those three up 91. Twenty nine the eighty seven thirty one the seven ninety two sixty two and the ninety one twenty twenty two. You thought I was going to miss that one, but I remembered.

So if we add all those up, we get to the one thousand sixty two forty four similar to what we got up top, close to what we got up top, but slightly different due to rounding because Of course, all the tables, all these decimal numbers here, here, here and there are rounded to four digits and are not quite exact close enough for most decision making purposes. Of course, for decision making purposes such as this, it would be close enough given the fact that this is an estimate. But beware Of course problems and test questions that might get really picky to try to force you to use one method or another.

Conclusion

But finance practice, problem use in one note. Future value calculation compounded quarterly. Get ready. It's time to take your chance with corporate finance. Here we are in one note. If you have access to one note and would like to follow along. You're not required to. But if you would like to work in the tab on the left hand side, where in the practice problems area, and then down here in the nine three five future value compounded quarterly tab.

Also note that when using that one note, you might want to take a look at the immersive reader tool. Many of our chapters will have a related file down here in the text areas. Those being chapters of the chapters, chapters that can then be translated to multiple different languages and then listen to or read in multiple different languages, thereby being a good complement to the chapter tabs up top. Closing this back out, we're going have our information up, tap into that information into the blue area down below.

We're going to be looking at a future value calculation. The difference here being that we have the compounded quarterly as opposed to annually, and therefore need to be careful about the years that we're going to be using, as well as the percent that we'll use. We'll take a look at this with regards to a mathematical formula. We'll take a look at it with regards to a running balanced type of scenario or situation calculation. And then we'll take a look at it with an excel, how we might put this into Excel and then the tables on down below, starting with our formula. The formula is going to be the future value equals the present value times at one plus hour to the end. So we're looking for the future value of the one hundred and fifty investment five years at 16 percent.

And we'll start that down here. But we've got to recognize, Of course, that it's going to be compounded quarterly. That's going to be a tricky scenario. So we're going to break this down into our format in terms of a table. And we're going to be having The PJV Times, this whole thing in the outer column. And then we'll break out the one plus R to the N in the inter columns. So we have the present value of one hundred and fifty. So we start off with the present value, the one fifty. That would not change whether we have compounded quarterly or other kinds of compounding areas. Then we have the one plus hour to the end that we're going to calculate. So we have one plus R. This is where things get a little bit different, because the percentage up here is 16 percent. And we're doing this quarterly.

So note that normally when you hear percentages, they will be in terms of yearly percentages. And therefore, we're going to have to break them down to the period that will be covered for us. In other words, the percent that we use needs to be matched in the period that we're going to use. In this case, we're using quarterly periods every three months. And therefore, it would need to take that percent and divide it by four. So we would take that 16 percent point one six divided by four, and that would give us our four percent. So then if we take the one plus the four percent, I'm going to add that to one that's going to give us one point four or one hundred and four percent.

And then we're going to take that to the number of periods, the next area where some complications will arise, because we were given the periods in terms of years. But we are talking about periods in terms of our calculation, compounded quarterly every three month type of periods, every quarter of a year. Therefore, we're going to take our years, times four. And we're talking about 20 periods that are not yearly long, but quarterly long. So we have 20. So now we get the one OA4 to the power of 20. I'm going to pull out the scientific calculator here to do that in Windows. To do that, we're going to go to this tab on the left scientific calculator.

I'm going to say this is the one point over then to the power of KARET 20. That's going to give us two points: one, nine , one, one, two, three, and so on. This has been represented in a percentage format over here. And then if we take that amount now we have this, times this and multiply it times, we're going to say times the one hundred and fifty thousand. We get the three twenty eight six six eight point four seven about, which is here at three twenty eight six six seven point four seven UBB. So now let's take a look at it again this time. Let's do it like a running balance type of calculation. This is something that would be tedious to do if you didn't have a spreadsheet. But with a spreadsheet, it is not difficult to do. So we'll do our running balance.

How would that change? We're going to start at period zero where we have our one hundred and fifty thousand, and then we'll say in period one will multiply this out. Now, when we multiply this out and add the interest, we've got one hundred and fifty thousand, and the first period is going to be the time we could do it this way. Point one six for a yearly percent. That would give us twenty four thousand if it were for a year. But it's quarterly so I can take that yearly rate or amount divided by four. And that would give us our six thousand. That, to me, is the most intuitive way to. You do it when you're doing a calculation and trying to get the percent for a particular time when you use formulas, however, oftentimes you'll just change the order of that calculation.

You'll be thinking about the percent with regards to the period that is covered. In other words. Point one, six divided by four would give us the percent per quarter point 04. Note that typically when you're given the percentages, they give the percentages per year, because when you give the percent per year, you have a fairly large number. When you break down the percentages per quarter or per month or per day, you're going to get to some fairly small numbers. Therefore, we have the custom of providing it per year. Most of the time, if you need to break it down to some other period, then you can break it down to some other period in this format.

Also note that, Of course, in using Excel, that's not difficult to do because the Excel worksheet will then pick up those small numbers and calculate them, even if they don't show those small numbers. Whereas when you're doing this by hand, it becomes more tedious to use basically those small numbers for the calculations. So if I take that point over and I multiply it times the one hundred and fifty thousand, we would get these six thousand once again. If we take that six thousand and add it to the one hundred and fifty thousand, then we're now at the one fifty six thousand if I go one more period out. Now we're talking about another quarter. So we got another like three month type of period out. We're going to take that amount. I'm going to multiply it times two point one six the yearly rate again.

That's going to give us twenty four nine sixty, which would be for a year. Take that, then divide it by four. We get these six to four. Oh, that's six two four zero plus the one fifty six thousand would give us the one sixty two to forty. And we can continue on with this down. Note that it would be more tedious to do this by hand. But if you have Excel, this would be easier to do. It's going to be a longer table than we would have if it was four years here. Compounded yearly, because there are five years, there would be five compounding, is there. Now we have quarterly.

So it's a much longer type of table, but it does give us a good idea of how the interest will grow on that basis. And if you have Excel, it's not difficult to do a calculation such as that, because you can use the autofill feature or copying and pasting to do so. Let's go to the future value down. I mean, let's do the future value calculation within Excel. So this would be an Excel formula. How would the Excel formula differ if it was compounded yearly versus quarterly? So we'd have the future value kind of calculation. And then we've got the B for which is going to be the rate. So that rate then that we put in place, when you enter this into an Excel formula, you have to make sure that you're matching up the rate to the periods, the same rate per period.

So I'm going to take that rate and we would divide it by four, and that would give us the rate per period. Note once again that using Excel, I don't need to actually know what that rate is or type it in, because Excel will then calculate the the rate out out to what the actual rate is, even if it's multiple decimal points, even though I'm basically calculating it on the yearly rate. So Excel can work with those small numbers. Well, in other words, without having to do the rounding, that we would have to do with a calculator quite easily. And then KOMMA, we have the number of periods. We have five years.

They give us the periods in years, but we're compounding quarterly. Therefore, we took that number of periods, times four, to give us the full amount and then comma. We then have the present value that's going to be the one hundred and fifty which will once again give us that three twenty eight six six four forty seven. Also note that you want to be careful when people discuss different compounds in different compounds like a yearly versus quarterly versus monthly, because note what we did here when we're compounding quarterly, I took this yearly rate and we broke it down to a quarterly rate.

And we took the years, Of course, and broke them down to the number of periods on a quarterly basis. If someone was to take the same information and say, we're going to we're going to go from a yearly compounding and quarterly compounding, and they didn't change the rate, meaning they gave the same rate that would would be the yearly rate as as the same rate that we would use for a quarterly rate. We would have a drastically different result. And we will do some comparisons with annual versus compounding quarterly versus compound in, I believe, monthly in a future chapter. So you can kind of compare and contrast those.

Just note again that when you change from going from compound yearly to monthly or quarterly, how are you going to be representing this percentage? Are you using the same percent as if it's the same yearly percent, then use the same rate for the quarterly percent, or you break this percentage down to the relative time periods in your comparisons? Any case will. Take a look at that later. If we do this with a table time, we have to be careful with the tables as well, because these tables down here do not represent yearly or any particular period. They just represent periods of compounding and the related interest rates. So up here, we have five and 16. But the periods that are going to be compounded are five times four or 20.

And then the 16 divided by four or the four. So if we go down below, then I have to make sure I'm looking at four and 20. So I'm looking at four and twenty four and twenty. And that's going to give us two points, one nine one one. There's the two point one nine one one one hundred and fifty thousand times two point one nine one one gives us the three to eight six six five, which is approximately the three to eight six six eight that we had up top. Also note that when you're looking at different kind of compounding options using a table, if you if you're doing like a book problem and you're restricted to the use of a table, the book problem will typically have to restrict the numbers that they're going to give you to some degree, because the tables you can see down here will typically be representing percentages for whole number percentages.

Meaning if there's a decimal percent, it's typically not on the table and you will not be able to be as exact with the table usages. So if you're breaking a problem down, they're going to have to use some intervals that will divide out evenly. So that might, you know, make it make the problems a little bit easier, make it a little bit more. You'll be able to expect what you were going to expect with the percentages if they're going to force you to use the tables. Also note that the years will be somewhat limited as well, because when you go from years to different time frames, like quarters or months, then this number is going to get quite large. And the tables, as you can see, go down to this one goes down to 50 periods. And when you're talking about months, those periods, you know, you can go past fifty periods quite easily. So tables will, Of course, limit the types of calculations that you can have. But many times book problems will utilize the tables to restrict people from using things like financial calculators.

www.ingramcontent.com/pod-product-compliance
Lightning Source LLC
Chambersburg PA
CBHW071911210526
45479CB00002B/366